Shell Collecting Made Simple

With best wishes

Graham Saunders

Graham Saunders

Published by

MELROSE BOOKS

An Imprint of Melrose Press Limited
St Thomas Place, Ely
Cambridgeshire
CB7 4GG, UK
www.melrosebooks.com

FIRST EDITION

Copyright © Graham Saunders 2008

The Author asserts his moral right to
be identified as the author of this work

Cover designed by Matt Stephens

ISBN 978-1-906050-28-3

All rights reserved. No part of this publication may be reproduced, stored in a retrieval system, or transmitted, in any form or by any means electronic, mechanical, photocopying, recording or otherwise, without the prior permission of the publishers. This book is sold subject to the condition that it shall not, by way of trade or otherwise, be lent, re-sold, hired out or otherwise circulated without the publisher's prior consent in any form of binding or cover other than that in which it is published and without a similar condition including this condition being imposed on the subsequent purchaser.

Printed and bound by:
Biddles, King's Lynn, Norfolk.

Topics

Introduction ... 1

Objectives ... 1

Nomenclature ... 2
    Taxonomic Systems ... 2
    Deciding Where to Collect ... 3

Environs ... 3
    Strandline ... 3
    Drift Line ... 4
    Run Off Channels ... 4
    Lagoons ... 4
    Estuaries ... 6
    Rock Reefs - Hard Rock - Soft Rock ... 6
    Hard clay ... 6
    Peat ... 7
    Mud ... 7
    Sand ... 7
    Weed Beds and Weed Covered Sublittoral Rock ... 9
    Small Weed ... 9
    Zostera Beds ... 9

Gravel - Shingle 10
Boulders 10
Modiolus Beds 11
Posidonia Beds 11
Kelp Beds 11
Coreline Algae 11
Hard Coral 12
Soft Coral 12
Sponges 12
Floating Driftwood 13
Ex-Pisces 13
Ex-Astropecten 13
Larger Shells 13

Opportunites 14
Oil Spills – Detergent kills 14
Fishermen's Waste 14
Fishmongers and Markets 14
Scallop Factories 14
Hermit Crabs 15
Dredged Landfill 15
Beach "Nourishment" 15
Harbour Repairs 15
Coastal Civil Engineering 15
Boats Beached for Maintenance 15
Beached Crab Boats 15
Restaurants 16
Aquaria 16
Shallows at Night 16
Baited Traps 16

Shell Collecting Made Simple

Collecting Methods 17
    Keeping Specimens Alive for Observation 18
    Hazards – Risks to Avoid 19

Examples of Recommended Labels 20

Cleaning Shells 21

Preserving Specimens 23
    Transporting Specimens 24
    Data to Record 25
    Conservation – How Much Damage am I Doing? 26
    Equipment 27
    Molluscan Provinces 29
    Exotic Shells 29
    Values – Does Rarity Have a Price? 30
    Shell Clubs 31
    Museums 31
    Learned Societies 32
    Exchanging 32
    Literature and Identification 33
    What is an Expert? 33
    Gastronomy – Can I Eat it? 34
    Taxonomic Systems – The Names Used and Why 35

Marine Charts – How to Interpret Them 39
    Shore Profiles 40

Animal Diagrams 41

Microshells ... 43

Dredge Options ... 44

Sea Areas ... 46

Sea Areas Map ... 47

Information ... 48
    The Conchological Society of
        Great Britain and Ireland ... 48
    The British Shell Collectors' Club ... 48
    The Malacological Society of London ... 49

Plates to Assist Identification ... 50

Potential in the UK ... 95

About the Author ... 99

Glossary ... 101

Index ... 103

Introduction

New shell books are written and re-written every year but none seems to meet the requirements of an enthusiastic novice who takes a serious but not necessarily scientific interest in the British fauna before widening interests to include exotic species. Currently available books are targeted at a casual juvenile readership. Beyond these there are only publications of the "learned societies" and clubs. These tend to be expensive, difficult for a newcomer to understand and hard to obtain. Periodically, expensive "coffee table" type books are produced. They *look* good. Some sell and the residue are remaindered cheaply.

Books published overseas sometimes include part of our fauna though they usually have a bias towards the more "showy" southern species and tend to be expensive and, again, are not easily available.

I am setting out to produce something inexpensive, functional and relevant. This is the book I needed 50 years ago!

Objectives

This book aims to provide an illustrated guide to the species likely to be found in the waters around the British Isles. Latin names will be provided in italics with common English names where these are available. I cannot recommend the use of common names as they usually cover a group of similar shells and not just one species.

I am writing for the casual holiday collector on the assumption that many readers will be children but that children are actually just as intelligent as adults though with less experience and more learning capacity. Ideally this is the first phase of a project to cover three different levels of information and geographic range.

Phase two would be a more comprehensive reference tool for the dedicated British or European collector, progressing to an identification guide with illustrations covering the molluscan fauna of the entire Eastern Atlantic but will I live long enough to complete them? Probably not! Ironically the last two actually started first but it is a moving target and a weekly updated internet site may be the answer.

For those who are interested in some of the basic scientific background I will include an outline of basic concepts such as species and how the nomenclature works and, as far as is possible, I will reduce this to plain English. I will also explain what the key words and most common technical terms mean.

My hidden agenda is to fast track a new generation of effective researchers and recorders.

Nomenclature

Taxonomic Systems

The names used in the few available publications have been out of date for many years. An appendix of taxa (names) extracted from the 1991 list published by the National Museums of Scotland by Smith and Heppell is adopted as the best now realistically available. The most frequently encountered synonyms (invalid names) are listed and each species will have a couple of lines of supporting notes. These will be index linked to the illustrations.

Deciding Where to Collect

For an absolute beginner the easy option is a beach where sand is depositing rather than eroding, during a Neap tide rather than a Spring tide. You have more time with sand exposed and the shells washing up are more likely to be empty. On-shore winds tend to wash in more live material but also a lot of dead weed. If there are offshore rocks or a hard substrate, the variety of species will be greater. Shores with some shelter from the prevailing winds are best. Bays with rock pools and weed will have limpets and snails (Gastropods), which will usually be alive or hosting hermit crabs. Nearly all shores will have some shells but do not try to tackle a mud flat until you have gained more experience.

Environs

Strandline

On a rising tide, the incoming waves push loose material up the beach. On a normal shelving beach, material deposits at the highest point that the waves reach. Shells found here bleach quickly in the sun but some fresh material is deposited if you get to it in time. Under normal conditions, most live material reaching the strand line is weak or dying. Collecting here has less environmental impact than collecting shells where they normally live. *Ensis* have a high mortality here. Storms can throw up large shells though much found here may be damaged. Consider using liquid paraffin to restore the colour of dead but undamaged material. Wash all material in fresh water before storing.

Drift Line

Wave action and long shore drift has a sorting effect. Shell debris tends to form a fairly narrow band of a different colour to the rest of the beach. Where tidal action is normal, there is usually only one major band but where there are more complex high tides caused by currents sweeping round our islands to meet up after travelling different distances to arrive at the same place, you get multiple lines. Empty fresh dead material as well as some live material is deposited in this way. Check any darker areas for microshells, skimming the top centimetre of the most promising areas for sorting at leisure under magnification. Examine kelp holdfasts for Blue-rayed Limpets and small *Musculus*.

Run Off Channels

At high tide, sand absorbs huge quantities of water. When the tide falls it drains out again. If the sand reservoir is big, springs form and cut sweeping erosion channels as they run down to the sea. Surface burrowers wash out, often in large numbers, and are swept along. Shell Bay on Herm is an excellent example where on spring lows, even *Lutraria angustior* may be exposed, as well as many *Venerids*, *Glycymeris* and *Dosina*. Watch out for the occasional *Naticid* here.

Beware quick sands, as they can exist in these conditions. Swim out of it if caught. Wading is dangerous or impossible. You just fall through sandy water till you hit the rock substrate below.

Lagoons

Saline lagoons are scarce in the United Kingdom. The Fleet behind the Chesil Bank in Dorset is the only significant one I am familiar with and this has a number of species typical of southern waters. The Fleet contains a range of habitats that are constantly evolving. There have been past attempts to establish commercial oyster and *Mercenaria* cultivation in some areas. After fishermen have dug bait, *Loripes lacteus* wash out of the sand. Deep below the sand in stagnant areas, *Scrobicularia plana* may be found. In the tidal channel between the causeway and the Chesil can be found exceptional *Litorina rudis*. The most exciting material is less obvious as many species exist mainly in the under-gravel streams that are pumped through the Chesil bank by wave action. Between the pebbles, in virtual darkness, will be found Chitons typical of much deeper water. *Caecum* species which normally live in Spain, *Turbonilla*, *Emarginula* and a host of unusual bivalves and microshells which are difficult to find elsewhere. Under dead *Zostera* at the top of the tide, you may find an abundance of *Truncatella*. *Paludinella* exist within the gravel but are difficult to see. Try thrusting a stick into the pebbles then examining it carefully. Run your fingers through the top few inches of wet pebbles. If *Cingula* are there, they will stick.

Near the Moonfleet vast quantities of *Akera bulata* swarm in the mud. There are huge drifts of dead material with abundant *Rissoa ventricosa*, *Cerastoderma glauca* and *Abra nitida*.

The inner and outer shores of lagoons often have quite different communities of species. As salinity may be higher at the mouth of the lagoon than at the head, there can be a series of different types of habitat and populations over a few kilometres.

Estuaries

Estuaries and their associated sand and mud flats have huge beds of common bivalves. Try digging and sieving for smaller bivalves. Cockle beds are often commercially exploited. Check the high water mark for brackish water species. Some estuaries have tidal bores so watch your timing. Where there are *Mytilus edulis* concentrations (possibly farmed) look for parasitic *Brachystoma*.

Rock Reefs – Hard Rock – Soft Rock

Every type of rock has its own fauna. Even granite boulders in surf host *Patella* and *Littorina* and small crevices provide shelter for *Mytilus*. The small white form of *Nucella lapillus*, which preys mainly on barnacles, can survive here but live specimens often look eroded.

Hard Clay

Most interesting at very low water, these expanses of apparently solid grey clay or shale are an ideal habitat for boring bivalves such as *Pholas*, *Barnea* and *Petricola*. There are usually also surface populations of *Littorina*, *Nucella* and sometimes *Buccinum*. Stones in gulleys may have Chitons on their underside. Loose weedy rubble often has several species of *Gibbula* in substantial numbers. On spring low tides, look for areas where there is a thin coating of sand over the clay. You will see countless trails where sea snails have ploughed by. When you walk you may see jets of water as bivalves retreat into their burrows. Carefully split some of the clay laterally and you will expose the burrows without breaking their shells. You can find other species in empty holes. Following fault lines in the clay live the young of *Nereid Ploychates* worms (fishermen call them ragworms). These are the prey species for *Turridae*, which rest under sands nearby and are sometimes exposed by wave action. Turrids are often intensely coloured when fresh but fade when dead and exposed to light. Offshore this substrate will produce *Calliostoma, Buccinum, Lacuna* and, if far enough north, *Neptunea*.

Peat

Intertidal peat beds are often an ideal habitat for boring bivalves and you have a good chance of getting the shell out undamaged.

Mud

Although littoral mud flats may have millions of small species such as *Hydrobia* and numerous bivalves, sublittoral mud produces a more diverse fauna and the largest specimens of species such as *Akera bullata, Philine aperta* and *Haminoea*. Some large bivalves can be found in mud. Obtain a wedge of black mud from the bottom of an unpolluted harbour, put it at one end of a plastic box and wait. As the water drains out, the inhabitants move downhill. It is interesting to observe how mobile even small bivalves can be and the trails in the mud demonstrate different modes of locomotion.

Sand

If the area is at all sheltered, this is a prolific habitat for bivalves, which can exist in astronomical numbers. Weaker specimens are washed out alive by wave action and are deposited in the drift lines. Some species, which have long siphons, will be buried several inches below the surface of the sand. Many are normally sublittoral and may only be accessible at spring low tides. Remember that some species can survive at the top of the beach where the sand is only covered for a few hours on each tide. Others can even cope with conditions above high water mark for short periods. Look for siphon holes in the sand and be prepared to dig. In sheltered shallow water, look for *Venus* shells and cockles half buried and the trails of *Nassarius* which are scavengers. Watch out also for the predators such as the *Naticids*. *Epitonium* bury themselves in the sand near sea anemones.

On the beach: not all beaches have shells on them but most do if only we can see them. If time is limited, look first at the parts where arcs of detritus can be seen. If there is a series of drift lines, try the lowest one first. Work over each stretch twice to take advantage of the difference in the way the light falls. From each direction, the light will profile different material. The ratio may be as high as five to one. Searching with your back to the sun is usually best. Where sand is covered by shallow water, look for surface tension dimples indicating objects below the surface. The reflection anomaly may locate a clear or sand coloured specimen.

Shell Sand/Grit: wave action has a sorting effect. Skim samples from the top one or two centimetres in the lower or middle drift line, discarding the more obvious stones and rubbish. Drain it in a strong cloth bag. At home split it wet with a medium sieve. Throw nothing away. Sort the coarse batch first under a very strong light. Use a strong hand lens such as a jewellers' loupe or a low power microscope, examining small samples on a contrasting surface, using a sable hair paintbrush to pick up individual specimens. The microscopic scales on the hairs grip most specimens, but dampen the tip of the brush if it is not working when dry. Artificial fibres are less suitable. Do not attempt to sort by species at this stage. Look at every grain or you will miss several species because all the time your brain is attempting to prioritise the data received from the eye. This seems daft but has been demonstrated by setting a series of experts to sort the same batch using the usual quick skim method. Their lists are incomplete and not identical. When wading birds predate molluscs, the same thing can happen. The bird's brain "locks on" to a one colour or one shape when food is plentiful.

Weed Beds and Weed Covered Sublittoral Rock

Weed Washings: take a large plastic bag into the water and agitate weed inside it so that any molluscs fall free into the bag. This works well with small weed covered stones. Remove and release fish, crabs, shrimps and any obvious juveniles. Try passing a flour sieve through the vegetation against the flow of any current, using a curving upward motion. If at all possible, sort it in shallow water and put back what you do not need, alive.

Small Weed

This often hosts a wide variety of microshells and juveniles of larger species, which seek other habitats when adult. Some molluscan species prefer a particular type of weed. Some species can only be found live in this habitat. Without detatching the clumps, shake the weed in the water over a fine sieve.

Zostera Beds

Tricolia, Jujubinus and certain *Rissoa* species can be sieved from sheltered *Zostera* beds. Work against the current, taking care not to permanently damage the plants, which may not re-establish if uprooted. Do not try to weed wash *Zostera* as you will do too much damage.

Gravel – Shingle

While at first sight this looks a totally hostile habitat, in sheltered areas, small species can live between the stones and *Osilinus* and *Littorina* will graze surface algae. Where there is a flow of water through the gravel a very complex community of invertebrates can exist. Some of the species are usually found offshore. There may be Chitons, *Kellia*, *Sphenia*, *Turtonia*, *Emarginula*, *Tectura*, *Cingula* and *Littorina*, often in astronomical numbers. Try running your fingers through any wet pebbles on the landward side of banks. *Cingula* are sticky and will remain on your fingers if they are present. *Paludinella* are also sticky but live deeper in the gravel. In the few places where they exist, they can be found by driving a stick into pebbles. They attach to the stick but are not easy to see. Offshore gravel shoals often have populations of large bivalves. These attract *Natica*. To get offshore gravel samples, one normally has to dredge or bribe scuba divers.

Gravel Banks: If you find a sheltered gravel bank, with well-rotted seaweed at the high water mark, move it and check the detritus below. Dig down several inches. You may find *Truncatella* or *Pseudophytina*.

Boulders

Boulders are often in the most hostile environments such as surf on open beaches or at the base of cliffs where they are scoured by wave-swept shingle. Some specialist *Littorina* can cope with this as can *Patella vulgata* and *Nucella lapillus* though they are generally seriously abbraided. If crevices provide enough shelter, *Mytillus edulis* can settle though they tend to be small here. In more sheltered positions weeds will cover the boulders and *Osilinus* and *Gibblua* will be found together with numbers of smaller species.

Modiolus Beds

Although *Modiolus* may be found intertidally in mud, it is more likely that they will be in deeper water on a gravel substrate. Their shells gape and the byssus attaches to any solid object nearby, including shells. The gaping shell closes on any falling object, for example, a fishing hook or pirk and the mass can be raised.

Posidonia Beds

Posidonia needs warmer water than *Zostera*. It hosts larger species of *Gibbula* and *Tricolia*.

Kelp Beds

These brown weeds are the preferred host of *Helcion*. The translucent thin-shelled variety lives on the flat leaves, while the heavier form burrows in the root holdfasts. Check all detached clumps washed ashore.

Coreline Algae

Sometimes referred to as "maerl" this normally forms beds offshore and is one of our richest habitats with *Aporrhais*, Turrids, *Turritella*, *Acanthocardia* and a host of interesting smaller species. It is usually only accessible by dredging or from fishermen's waste. In warmer waters you may get small *Bursa* and *Murex* with *Strombus* and small *Cypraea* species if you are in the right area. Coralline rubble, dredged in a sheltered area, may produce spectacular Pectens, Buccinids, Epitonids and *Marginella* species. Usually there are also a wide variety of bivalves such as *Glycymeris* and *Venus*. *Cypraecassis* and *Terebra* are scarcer as are the larger *Mitridae*. You could get almost anything here if you persist.

Hard Coral

As only solitary corals inhabit our colder waters, you will normally only meet with these in the tropics. Offshore forests of small coral "trees" are the favourite habitat of *Cypraea achatidea*, which has been reported from as far North as western Portugal. Not many molluscs prefer live coral as a habitat although *Coralliophila* actually eat coral polyps but the shelter provided by dead coral slabs and rubble, particularly if just inside an outer reef where oxygen and nutrient levels are high, can provide a spectacular assortment of families and species. Virtually every dead shell will host a hermit crab. Under the largest slabs you may find *Charonia*, large *Cypraea*, *Latirus* and big Trochids. Bivalves will excavate holes in dead coral or even the thicker shells of other species.

Soft Coral

In the tropics, many *Ovulidae* or *Trividae* species prey on soft corals. *Cyphoma* graze sea fans and sea whips, which colonise sublittoral reef flats.

Sponges

While some species of sponge do not seem an attractive habitat for mollusca, some larger *Cypraea* live within them or feed on them. Some Pectens live embedded in them. *Bittium* tunnel in certain sponges. Specimens from this source are usually perfect.

Floating Driftwood

Floating wood may have crossed the Atlantic. Examine it carefully for signs of shipworms or other "passengers".

Ex-Pisces

A number of the larger fish will eat molluscs and some very attractive small Pectens have been recovered from the stomachs of cod. Some of the rarer deep water *Cypraea* were originally described from material retrieved from fish guts.

Ex-Astropecten

Some starfish species ingest small molluscs. I have obtained material from this source by exchange but the concept of eviscerating a starfish on the off chance that shells might be recovered, does not appeal to me!

Larger Shells

The algae growing on the backs of the large *Patella* and *Haliotis* are worth checking for micro shells. Small species of *Crepidula* are often to be found on the opercula of the large *Fasciolaria*.

Opportunities

Oil Spills – Detergent Kills

After an oil spill has been cleaned up, there are medium term casualties weakened or killed by the detergents and these wash ashore over time.

Fishermen's Waste

Look in weed from net cleaning or detritus dumped from boat cleaning.

Fishmongers and Markets

Interesting strangers turn up amongst molluscs sold for human consumption. Look for *Colus* amongst *Buccinum*. Getting data can be difficult! The trade is international. We export to France and Spain.

Scallop Factories

A scallop factory is an installation where dredged material from offshore is processed to separate edible scallop meat. Lots of other species turn up. Factories are usually located where public health regulations are lax.

Hermit Crabs

These are more mobile than living shells and may carry them into traps or walk then into shallow water.

Dredged Landfill

Dredged material used for landfill can include spectacular deep water material.

Beach "Nourishment"

Some local authorities move sand to create beaches where there is normally erosion. Waves have a sorting effect, concentrating useful material.

Harbour Repairs

Hunks of stone removed from the water are often covered with weed with lots of shells in it. Borers such as *Barnea* will be found in soft rock.

Coastal Civil Engineering

Areas cut off and dried out should be investigated for stranded shells.

Boats Beached for Maintenance

When a boat has been in the water for such a long time that the antifouling paint no longer works, it is beached for cleaning. The covering of weed normally has shells in it.

Beached Crab Boats

Shells crawl over the traps and fall off when the trap hits the deck. They end up dead in cracks and corners. Remove them discretely without upsetting the owner.

Restaurants

There is the menu and the window display to check. You may need to tip extravagantly. The restaurant often has a close relationship with local fishermen who can be persuaded to save shells for you.

Aquaria

Some dealers in saltwater fish also have shells. These usually die before they are sold and can be obtained at lower prices.

Shallows at Night

Lots of snails are nocturnal. With a strong light, trails can be seen in mud or sand. Be careful!

Baited Traps

Hermit crabs and scavengers are attracted to a trap or drop net with fish offal.

Collecting Methods

Many shells on the strand line will already be empty and just need washing off in fresh water. The most obvious will probably be bivalves and separated rather than in joined pairs. Anything still alive is probably not strong enough to survive or it would not be there. Cleaning will be necessary. If you see a lot of small shells in the drift line, skim it with a sieve, rinse out the sand and throw away any obvious rubbish. Drain off water. Sort it later under magnification. Look under stones of all sizes. Those in a stable environment resting on other stones are best. Examine both the stone and the substrate for Gastropods and Chitons (flat segmented and oval in shape) and any crevices for small Bivalves. Where there is an assortment of seaweed in sheltered water, shake it in water over a flour sieve or put some in a plastic bag with some water and shake the whole thing. Amazing things usually fall to the bottom. Some have shells! Return all juveniles and unwanted life forms to the sea. Follow rocks down from the "splash zone" to below low water mark checking crevices. Some *Littorina* and Limpets (*Patella*) are very hardy and different species adapt to successive zones down the shore.

Some limpets will actually wear a cavity in flat, soft or porous rocks. Sheltered shallows are always worth checking for the trails left by *Nassarius*, *Acteon* or hermit crabs. Bivalves often lie on the surface. Flats of hard grey clay or shale may be riddled with boring bivalves. Turrids hunt where thin drifts of sand overlay the clay. On real "Spring Lows", even *Calliostoma* and *Buccinum* may be found here. Keep your eyes open for the unexpected in unlikely places.

Keeping Specimens Alive for Observation

Molluscs are usually very hardy and will survive in seawater in a shallow tray without food for several days. You can observe them for a few hours without harming them but they may take the opportunity to kill each other. In the process they may drill holes in each other's shells, reducing their desirability as specimens. Compare the siphons of the bivalves and the foot and tentacles of the Gastropods. Each species is different. Small species should be viewed with a lens for full appreciation. Sketch what you see and take notes of the colours. Anything returned to the sea should be placed in a similar habitat so it can survive. If you buy live shells from a fishmonger for your collection and there are broken ones, put these back in the sea. They can repair themselves almost overnight.

Hazards – Risks to Avoid

Be aware of time and tide. Be sure you can get back safely. Quick sand and soft mud can be swum out of but trying to stand and walk just gets you deeper into trouble. Rubber soled shoes and at least one glove reduce many risks. Too much broken glass ends up on beaches. Sea anemones, which cannot harm a dry hand, are quite capable of stinging soft damp skin. Sea urchin spines can break in the skin and have to be dissolved out with vinegar. There may be spined weaver fish in summer, in the South. Conger eels in holes may bite the unwary. Crab claws can do a lot of damage! Do not touch bristle worms. Some jelly fish sting and a few are actually dangerous. Last but not least are sunburn and sunstroke, which can both take the fun out of collecting. The head and back of legs are high-risk areas. Wear a hat. Cover up. Do not put your faith entirely in sun blocking creams. If mosquitoes, sand flies or horseflies (called Cleggs in Scotland) are vicious, wear a wet suit.

Examples of Recommended Labels

washed from red and brown weed at 0.5 m between reefs, Sandsfoot, Portland Harbour, Dorset
G D Saunders   September 1992

dredged in rubble, Porto Grande Sao Vincente, Republic of Cabo Verde, Andrade 78

Blank for unsorted batches

Chlamys varia
(Linne, 1758)
trawled, Baie de St Brieuc
Brittany France, 1993
M Le Quement

Exchanged but originally from fisherman

ALGOA BAY SPECIMEN SHELLS
P.E.
P.O. BOX 804
Port Elizabeth
6000
South Africa

Family	CYPRAEIDAE
Genus	CYPRAEA
Species	FUSCORUBRA
Author	SHAW, 1909
Locality	CAPE PENINSULA (WEST), S.W. CAPE PR.
Date	1993
Remarks	ALIVE ON REEF, AT 40M.

CYPRÆIDAE   D·35
Cyprœa asellus
Linnaeus, 1758
Intertidal under rock,
Rameswaram, Tamil Nadu,
India
(Col. native person, 2003)

Commercial labels

Epitoniidae
Epitonium occidentale
Nyst, 1871
in sponge at 80 ft
dredged 120 miles E.S. East
of St Augustine Florida
p.m. 14 April 1981.
G.D. SAUNDERS

Full data except for geographic detail

35°20'N 24°17'E Georgiopolis CRETE
under rocks 1-2m by causeway to
shrine. GDS 18 Sept 1987

35°30'N 23°30E new harbour near
Trachilos CRETE not on map under
stones and in weed of sheltered
bay. GDS 24 Sept 1987

35°17'N 23°30'E Paleochora CRETE
sheltered rocky bay 1-3m
G D Saunders 24 Sept 1987

35°22'N 25°25'E Hersonissou CRETE
under stones in shallows
G S Saunders late Sept 1987

With map references for later sorting and re-labelling

Genus	: Alvania
species	: mediolittoralis
auteur	: Gofas, 1989
localiteit	: Ponta Delgada, Isl. of Sao Miguel, Azores 91/88

A good exchange label

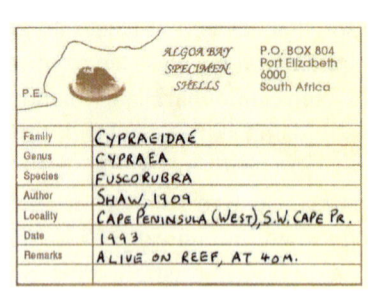

Cleaning Shells

You found it on the beach. There is no animal but it is covered in barnacles and weed encrustation. Wash it in fresh water, drain it then place in a strong luke warm chlorine bleach solution for a couple of hours.

There are few worse smells than rotting sea life. Bivalves can be scraped out with a wooden or plastic spatula or soaked for a limited period in alcohol or formalin then dried. It is also possible to dehydrate them by a series of short microwave bursts, preserving the entire animal. The microwave can also be used to blow out the animal from a difficult gastropod. The steam pushes from the narrow end. Wrap kitchen paper over the items being microwaved to avoid smelly splatter and the operculum will be easier to find afterwards. The operculum is the chitinous or ceramic plate used by the animal to close its aperture. It is part of the shell. Save it.

Snails generally need more cleaning. Is there a periostracum to be preserved? If not, more choices are available. They may need soaking in a solution of warm bleach to loosen encrustations before removing weed with a stiff brush or flaking away calcium and barnacles with a dental tool or similar. Do not start with a treasured rarity. Practise on an old or broken specimen. Only adults should experiment with hydrochloric acid (sold in the UK as "spirits of salts"). Many good shells have been damaged by over enthusiastic use of acid, but there are times when it is the only way to remove a very thin film of calcium. A half second may be all that is required. Rinse immediately, remembering that acid burns flesh and stainless steel draining boards as well!

If you are boiling shells before hooking out the animal remains, remember to raise or lower the temperature slowly or the surface may craze. Flush it out as soon as the water cools. The liquid may have become corrosive. If you resort to "rotting out" change the water very regularly or it will spoil glossy surfaces. When cleaned and dried, specimens may be dressed with medicinal paraffin oil to restore lost surface layer oil and colour. Cowrie collectors apply a wipe of silicone wax and keep the specimens in darkness to delay inevitable fading. Colours with a blue component almost always fade with time. The shells remain beautiful but violets fade to reddish brown. *Janthina* are an exception.
Freezing is only safe for certain types of shell. Porous varieties delaminate if frozen.

Consider the scientific value of peripherals such as the operculum and the periostracum. Do take the time to preserve the opercula, removing them before you put the shell in bleach. The periostracum covers the underlying colours of some shells and you will probably wish to display these but do not remove it from all your specimens. Different but closely related species can have distinctly structured periostracum quite critical for identification. There are differences in texture, density, scales, lines of hairs and so on. Oil the surface lightly before they dry out completely. Dried periostracum can flake off.

Preserving Specimens

Once a shell is superficially clean, wash it well in fresh water and dry it out of direct sunlight. When it is completely dry, consider whether it is necessary to refresh colour by replacing surface oils with liquid paraffin. Store in a dry, dust free place, dark if possible, but certainly out of direct light. Cotton wool is the traditional padding. One can get unfortunate chemical reactions with some foams and petrochemical derivatives. If plastic containers are used they reduce problems with airborne damp and acid emanations from wood.

Never EVER keep important specimens in oak cabinets or drawers unless the inside has been varnished. Acid permeates the air and will rot the specimens over time.

I know that important museums make just this mistake but the curator usually blames his predecessors and the specimens are expensive to change. Some experienced collectors dismiss the risk but it is not one I would take.

The vacuum containers that can be pumped out by hand enable you to boil at low temperatures. They are sold in gimmicky kitchen specialist shops. Pholads can be dehydrated intact using a series of short microwave bursts. Loosely wrap in clean kitchen towel paper, opening and turning between short bursts until dry. This preserves the whole thing. The microwave will also pop out most of a *Turritella* and recover those far in opercula. Cover!

Bluetac migrates! By all means use it for a short period for exhibitions but over time the volatile elements will move to the shell and leave a darker patch.

Salt has a rotting effect on microshells over time. Make quite sure they are free of it. Damp permits mould and bacteria to degrade the surface of cowries in particular.

Some collectors in tropical or subtropical areas have dehumidifiers in constant use. A few museums go to the extent of sealing their most important collections in a toxic gas environment. The safe access period for students is twenty minutes and by the end of that period, one is not feeling good. Light is the enemy of colour. If you must display it, make sure it is not irreplaceable!

Transporting Specimens

To transport shells alive for study, use very shallow water to maintain oxygen levels. Keep spare clean seawater separate for later use when it can be aerated. Do not mix carnivores and vegetarians for obvious reasons. Give Chitons a suitable stone to attach to or they will curl up and die.

Containers need to be watertight, preferably airtight, and uncrushable. If shells are dead and half cleaned, wash them in fresh water, drain them and immerse them in surgical spirit or formalin for a short time, drain them again and pack them in toilet paper in an airtight container. Deal with them as soon as practicable after you get home. Do not carry shells in formaldehyde in glass containers on aircraft or tube trains. I once broke one on the London Underground. These days they would think "Sarin", assume one is a terrorist, shoot first and ask questions later!

If you have something large and in spite of all your efforts, it still smells evil, pack it in commercial cat litter granules and wrap it in a series of sealed plastic bags, getting as much air out as you can first so it will not burst as the air pressure on the aircraft cabin changes. Small, uncleaned specimens can be transported in a "Vinsave" vacuum jar. These are not excessively expensive and you can get a lot of small shells in a litre. Wet sand samples are best initially drained in a cotton bag before putting them in labelled plastic. Rinse and dry them as soon as practicable.

If you have clean dry specimens, bubble plastic and cotton wool protect delicate shells. Always label the containers with normal data.

Data to Record

Ideal data includes notes on the habitat, the collecting point, date, depth of water, state of tide and the name of the collector. This transforms a shell from a bathroom ornament to a specimen of potential scientific value.

Some molluscs are parasites. If possible, identify the host organism. Some species live only in association with particular plants or animals.

If you have seen the living animal, sketch it and note the colours. If you see any specimens with eggs, why not photograph the whole scenario without killing. One can usually obtain what one needs without destroying two generations!

The definition of the locality may prove important later, so, if you are in remote areas where place names will mean little to a third party, give the best map grid reference available. There are population surveys attempting to map species distribution in our waters by 10 kilometre squares. The remotest areas are the ones with the fewest proper records.

Find a book which gives you the names of the commonest seaweeds as this information helps us to understand the relationships between species.

Some examples of label types are included in the information section. If a shell is identified at the time of collection, the importance of the labelling grows as it may prove to be uncommon or a first record for that area.

Conservation – How Much Damage am I Doing?

Most shells exposed on a beach are either dead or going to die in the very near future so one can collect here with a clear conscience. The strongest might survive if thrown back into deeper water but in general, only shells weakened by misfortune are deposited there. If there has been a large natural mortality of an interesting species, take as many good specimens as you can cope with. The population may take a while to recover and, with a lot of material in circulation, other collectors are less likely to molest the survivors. Never damage habitats as this affects future generations. *Zostera* (sea grass) beds are easily destroyed and regenerate slowly. Brown and red seaweeds die back in an annual cycle but regenerate quickly. If you turn stones, always replace them so eggs are not exposed to sunlight. Hermit crabs may be dazed by immersion for a while in soapy water, then rinsed out and released.

Only take home living material if you are sure you are capable of cleaning it properly and be certain that you have separated juveniles and surplus material from weed, washing quickly so they can be returned alive to their original environment. Take photographs of the living animals. You would be amazed how little is known of the actual animals of some species and you will be filling gaps in our education.

Equipment

Here is a list of all the collecting equipment you may eventually need. Some items are dangerous and need careful handling. Access to a first aid kit is also recommended!

Flour Sieve
Two mesh sizes – with and without handles.

Plastic Containers
Some wide mouthed with clip on, air-tight tops, smaller ones such as used 35mm film containers, recycled paint or plaster containers, large black plastic tray.

Cotton Bags
Strong enough to take four litres of wet sand, smaller ones to separate important finds which might damage or eat each other after capture.

Plastic or Nylon Bag
Must be very strong and waterproof to take drained but still wet bags – or a five gallon paint can with handle if preferred.

Trowel
Preferably narrow.

Garden Fork
Or follow bait diggers round!

Wrecking or Docker's Hook
A large steel hook with crossbar handle for turning large slabs and boulders.

Geologist's Pick or Brick Hammer
For extracting borers from rock – eye protection is also recommended!

Magnifying Glass or Jeweller's Loupe

Dental Tools
  For removing encrustation.

Surgical Spirit, Formalin, Glycerine
  1cm diameter plastic or wood Rod, cotton or tape – all useful in the preparation of Chitons.

Hydrochloric acid, medicinal liquid Paraffin Oil (some swear by baby oil), concentrated Bleach, Silicone Wax, Salt.

Face Mask and Snorkel
  For improved vision in the shallows. Glass Bottomed or clear Plastic Boxes are sometimes used by the geriatric but only the larger species are easily seen with them.

Dredge
  Hand or towable from boats.

Baited Drop Net
  To lower from piers to attract scavengers and hermit crabs.

Paint Brush
  Artist type with sable hair – artificial fibres are inadequate – for picking up microshells.

Admiralty Charts and Tide Tables
  For planning where and when to collect. Charts show rocks, depths and bottoms.

Vacuum Jar for dehydration
  Litre vacuum jars are made by Vinsave who normally sell wine preservers. You could put in the entire shell with animal and pump out the air. The water then boils away at room temperature and you then pump out the vapour. The entire specimen is then preserved intact.

Microwave Ovens
Can be used to blow out deep in remains or to dry and preserve entire bivalve animals.

Molluscan Provinces

This is a term used to indicate geographic areas containing communities of species largely particular to those areas. A few species are very adaptable and have ranges of distribution extending through several "provinces". Some species have been deliberately or accidentally introduced to new areas as a result of commercial activity and have become firmly established. Temporary climate shifts can result in rapid population changes. At the edge of ranges, some species do not breed successfully every year. Non-breeding individuals can grow to exceptional sizes. We are European province. In the Channel Islands, shells are starting to look different from their mainland equivalents but are treated as "British" for recording purposes.

Exotic Shells

Shells have been imported as curiosities and decorations for centuries and vast numbers are imported and sold by seaside shops. Fortunately many of these are by-products of human consumption. Interesting species can turn up amongst the junk but few will have reliable data. Buy these for their beauty but not for science. There are a couple of mail order or internet dealers in the UK and they have some excellent material, usually with reliable data. Some material can be expensive. There are normally two shows/conventions each year in the UK. Foreign dealers attend. There are many bargains to be had together with really expensive rarities. Foreign bourses are vast by our standards and attract thousands of collectors. Colours, shapes and sizes of many exotic species are spectacular. Fewer of the temperate water species are large and colourful.

Values – Does Rarity Have a Price?

In theory there is no such thing as a truly rare shell as a species must have a core population in order to survive. We tend to call species rare when we cannot access the places where they live. Some species live in areas seldom visited or in deeper waters not currently being dredged or trawled by anyone prepared to sell material to collectors. Value is built up from several factors such as the risks taken to obtain the shell, the difficulty in cleaning it, cost of transport, condition, quality, supply and demand. Although a lot of British shells are hard to obtain, the market is limited so values may be low although for certain attractive families international dealers may ask high prices and eventually get them. In some American States, tax breaks are available on donations of rare material to public museums. In return for multiple high value donation certificates, the controller of the material reaps more financial benefit than could be gained by selling to collectors at lower prices.

Some foreign families are valued highly because the supply has been very limited over the years. A rarity may suddenly reappear on dealers' lists but sometimes it does not pay to respond too quickly. The source may have a big quantity in his cellar and will not release them until he has maximised his profit. The price can drop from $2,000 each to $200 within a few months. Shells purporting to be the record holders for the largest of species may actually be the smallest of a series of spectacular specimens which are to be released over a period of time to achieve maximum profit. What price your moment of fame? Be very certain of what a shell is worth to you before you invest in a rarity. Specimen shell prices respond to the laws of supply and demand, just like everything else and the total number of specimen shells in collections increases each year. When buying a special shell, ensure that you have reliable data. Some data is deliberately obscured by collectors, who, for various reasons, feel it is essential to conceal their sources. This seriously devalues the specimens scientifically.

Shell Clubs

The British Shell Collectors Club is currently the only UK based club and smaller or Northern countries seem to have only one each. Overseas, things are different and many coastal cities have their individual clubs. Some of the richer ones fund university scholarships in addition to conducting monthly meetings and holding annual events such as public shows and bourses. The primary purpose of a club is to enable those with a shared interest to locate each other and exchange information and specimens. They may also organise field trips and contribute to the population surveys. As a club, they can purchase subscriptions to foreign magazines or jointly acquire expensive reference works. If the club is large enough it can publish its own magazine and host international shell shows. Until postage costs made it impracticable, the British club had a library of reference works. Meetings are an opportunity to recycle old collections.

Museums

The Natural History Museum (NHM) (formerly British Natural History Museum, BNHM) was chartered by Parliament as the repository of the National Collection, which is an accumulation of material gifted to the Nation over many years. It has secondary roles in curating it, supporting research and making displays available to the public (us). Some recent administrations have felt a need to entertain rather than just to educate us. Like most museums, they are understaffed, under funded and faced by insuperable conflicts of priorities. Only a tiny % of their holdings can be displayed but they are making the best of an impossible situation.

Learned Societies

These are clubs for well educated students, "experts" and active amateur enthusiasts who meet, exchange information and publish journals which are the usual vehicle for the formal description of newly recognised species and suitably vetted new scientific data and statistics. Some are incomprehensible to amateurs. The Malacological Society and the Conchological Society of Great Britain and Ireland are the principal ones working our area of interest.

Exchanging

Most exchanging is done by post. Collectors produce lists of their surplus material and send them to other collectors who are believed to have an interest. To avoid disappointment it is essential that both parties clearly indicate the condition and origins of what they are offering. Scarcity is relative as some species are common in some areas but seldom seen in others. If two exchangers are just starting, it may be possible to offer 5O different species with good data from each locality. In such circumstances, if a species was available in quantity, I would try to send a colour range and usually the exchange partner would try to do the same. Always remember that the resources of an area will be traded out after a few exchanges and you will need to find other partners. In an ideal world you need partners who collect their own material. It can be frustrating to send shells to Australia and get back commercial shells without data. Many almost certainly originated in India or the Philippines! If you are running out of decent material, do not be afraid to say so, as to send second rate material eventually loses you a friend.

Literature and Identification

Some useful books have been available in the past but are now out of print and thus difficult to obtain. They are all based on out dated taxonomy, subsequently revised and updated under the auspices of the National Museum of Scotland, so their use has serious drawbacks. There is no up to date reference work on the British Gastropods in a format of much use to the beginner, The "British Bivalve Seashells, A Handbook for Identification", by Norman Tebble, published for the Royal Scottish Museum by Her Majesty's Stationery Office, Edinburgh, published in 1966 is still worth tracking down. The two volumes of European Seashells by Poppe & Goto, published by Verlag Christa Hemmen, are well illustrated but not comprehensive for our area and I have a few reservations on their taxonomy.

What is an Expert?

In really crude terms an expert is a student who has more information than most of us. Not all information is reliable and with the passage of time, many assumptions have been treated as if they were facts. You bring fresh eyes to a science or hobby and you will see things that have never been adequately recorded in reference books. There are very few professional conchologists functioning in the United Kingdom at any given time. The subject is so vast that most are sooner or later forced to specialise in a particular family or environment.

Some "experts" just rework museum collections and study existing literature. The latter is of limited value unless the data is authenticated by current fieldwork. If you are in the right place at the right moment, you may learn at first hand things that experts have missed in decades of study. I had the good fortune to work for a couple of years within 200 metres of an interesting beach and checked the drift line for about 400 separate half hours during that time. There were the predictable seasonal variations in what washed ashore, but during that time, only four really significant records and observations were made. Twenty years later one of the gastropods, animal still preserved in alcohol, remains unidentified even to family level in spite of consultation of literature and experts. Learn from whoever is willing to teach, but remember the experts do not necessarily agree with each others' opinions and may not be prepared to communicate with each other for various reasons.

Gastronomy – Can I Eat it?

It is believed that no healthy mollusc, properly cooked, is actually poisonous though a few taste unpleasant or are too tough to chew unprocessed. Every species tastes different and some taste a lot better than others, commanding high prices. Huge quantities of Oysters, Clams, Scallops, Abalones, Cockles, Whelks, Conch and Winkles are consumed annually in the developed world, elsewhere, you eat anything you can get!

Taxonomic Systems – The Names Used and Why

The "*name game*". The only accepted system for naming species has been used since 1758 and is based on a form of Latin. It is bi-nomial with the first word indicating the family (usually called the Genus in scientific circles) and the second word being the specific name which is intended to clearly identify a specimen as a member of a particular gene pool, i.e. a "*Species*".

If a population seems to be distinct and not interbreeding with other populations, and no trace of an earlier valid description can be found, a student may select a single shell he regards as typical of that gene pool and base a description on it. If this is done properly and then published validly, it is designated the "*Holotype*". If there are other good specimens available in this same locality, they can be designated "*Paratypes*" and form part of a "*Type Series*". This enables specimens to be lodged at several museums etc for easier reference by other students. If you see a specimen labelled "*Topotype*" it has come from the same collecting point as the type material but is not a specimen used in the original descriptive process.

Prior to 1758 there was no consistent way of identifying life forms. Naturalists and auctioneers attempted to describe what they were writing about in their own languages with no common system. None of them were quite sure what others were dealing with. Science was largely in the hands of gifted amateurs or rich sponsors and collectors. Carl Linaeus laid down the foundations of the system we still use, although over the centuries there have been changes to recognise later research and discoveries. A Latin based system was used because it was the only common language of scholars and it has the added advantage of being a *dead* language. In theory, the meaning of the words would not change over the years! Conchology (shell collecting to us), is unfortunately one of those areas of study where there is no universally accepted exact definition of concept "*species*" and after two and a half centuries of acrimony, some uncertainties remain.

For a name (Taxon) to be valid it must have "***Priority***" and that means that no one else has validly described that population at an earlier date. However, there are more requirements to satisfy! Is the physical material on which the description was based all one species? The shells can look similar but actually be different. If the "***Type Series***" includes more than one species, the name becomes invalid. In some instances, the original description appears to have been based on a batch of shells rather than one in particular. If the batch is all one species the series are called "***Syntypes***". A later expert may designate one of these as a "***Lectotype***" on the assumption that that one is closest to the description. This is then an inferior substitute for an actual "***Holotype***". If the Type Series or the Syntypes subsequently prove to include more than one species, the naming and description are technically invalid and a later Taxon gets priority. Some examples, causing problems, are where eggs or sexual organs are different though adults look identical.

Some populations produce live young while others, again visually identical, lay eggs. Experts who rely on literature rather than field research are at a considerable disadvantage and their determinations are at risk. Most species communicate biochemically, using pheromones (complex chemical signalling), which enable them to tell who is who. If you are in the right place, at the right time, on the right day of the year, you can see them sort each other out in sequence. It seems to have evolved so that there is an interval between the mating of closely related species to reduce hybridisation.

After a species has been described and named, there is always the risk that examples of the same species, living in another place and under different conditions, will look sufficiently different for a later researcher to publish another description and name. When this happens the later name is called a "***Synonym***". Some authors get quite upset about this as their work is invalid and the suggestion is that they have not done their homework properly. There have been enough arguments for a ruling body to be necessary. The ICZNS (International Committee for Zoological Nomenclature) gives opinions or rulings in cases where something too irrational has come to pass!

In 1758, less was known of the relationships between species. Shells were grouped into families on the basis of very incomplete data and it transpired that there were far more families than anyone had imagined at the outset. New family names (***Genera***) had to be created and a lot of the species already described, had to be re-allocated to new Genera. When you see ( ) round the name of the author and the date of publication, it shows that we got it wrong the first time round, but this was the first validly published description of the species. The game continues as we learn more. A further development came with the introduction of books for public use. Most publishers, having a low opinion of the intellect of their target market, insisted that there should be English, or French etc names to go with the illustrations. The snag was that there were probably only about 150 common names extant so the author or the editor had to make them up. Utter chaos followed. There were attempts to anglicise the Latin taxa but only too often, the taxa they were translating were not the ones with priority. Worse, the same name is applied to different species in different places. Words mean different things to different people. One colloquial name will be applied to a series of quite unrelated species depending on where you happen to be at the time!

Most type material is in the care of national museums and should be available to serious students for comparison with potentially new material. This is an ideal that seldom works in practice because of human nature. Circumstantial evidence suggests that avarice overcomes conscience. Some original type material has been substituted, lost or mislaid. One refers to the shell labelled "***Holotype***" but is it? Does it look like the original illustration (if there was one)? If it does not, why not? Less cynical observers might say that the Author had only an elderly worn specimen and used artistic licence to construct a picture of how it might have looked when it was alive. I believe that this was very rare and that somewhere shells exist which match the original illustration and the Type is missing. Substitutions are not necessarily the result of villainy. I have sent material to a museum for comparison and have had a Paratype sent back to me in error. Professional researchers working for museums are not blameless. Their priority is the completion of their next publication, not the return of loan material. The attempts by one of the curators at the BMNH to retrieve study loans earned for her the international pseudonym of the *Dragon Lady* but I do not know what her success rate is! These problems remain unresolved.

Marine Charts – How to Interpret Them

Charts include such information as depth, seabed type, shoreline type and road access.

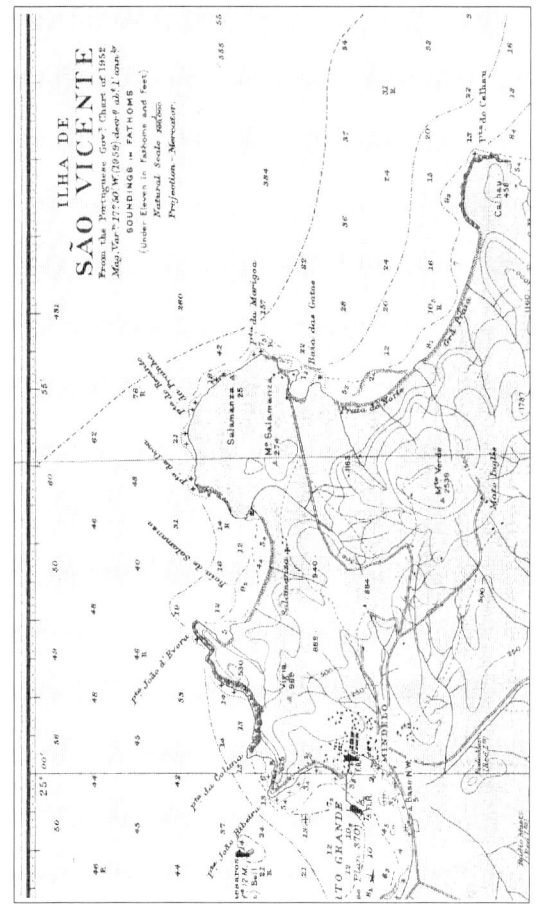

Favourable areas are bays with some shelter, with mixed sand and rocks at low tide.

Shore Profiles

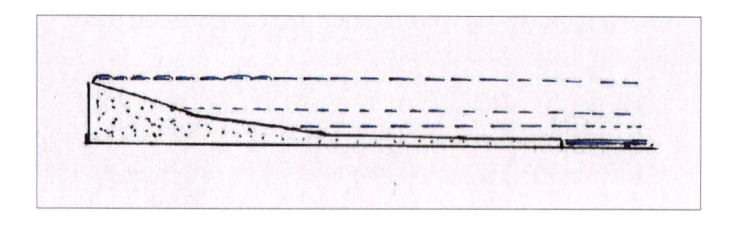

Sand Beach: some with dunes above
Top line: Spring high water
Second line: Neap high water
Third line: Neap low water
Lowest areas exposed at spring low water

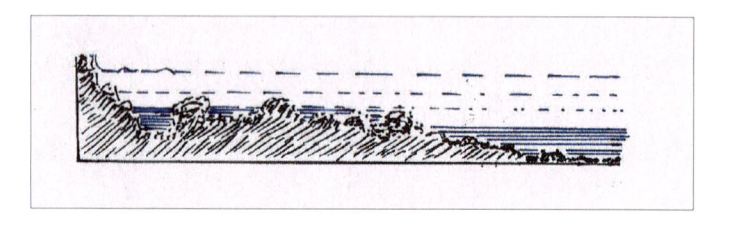

Rocky Shore: splash zone
Top line: Spring high water
Second line: Neap high water with rock pools
Third line: Neap low water with more rock pools then sublittoral stone

Shell Collecting Made Simple

Animal Diagrams

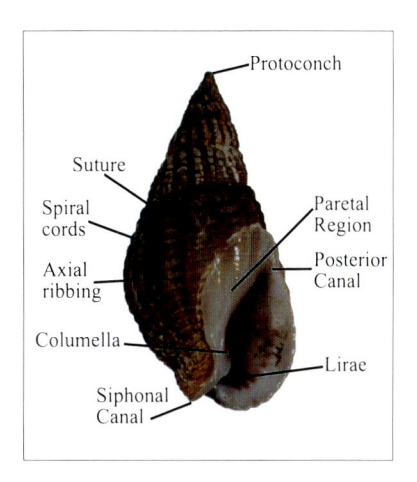

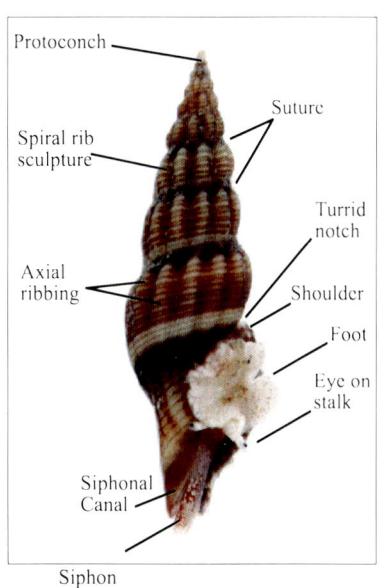

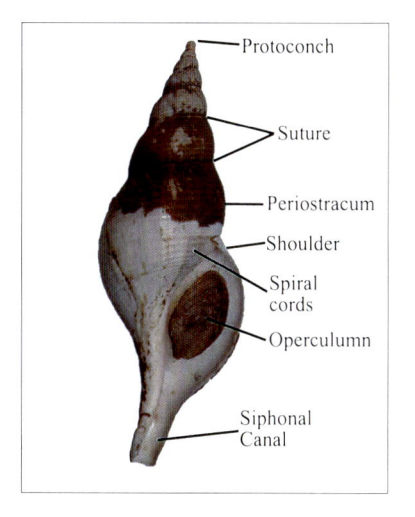

41

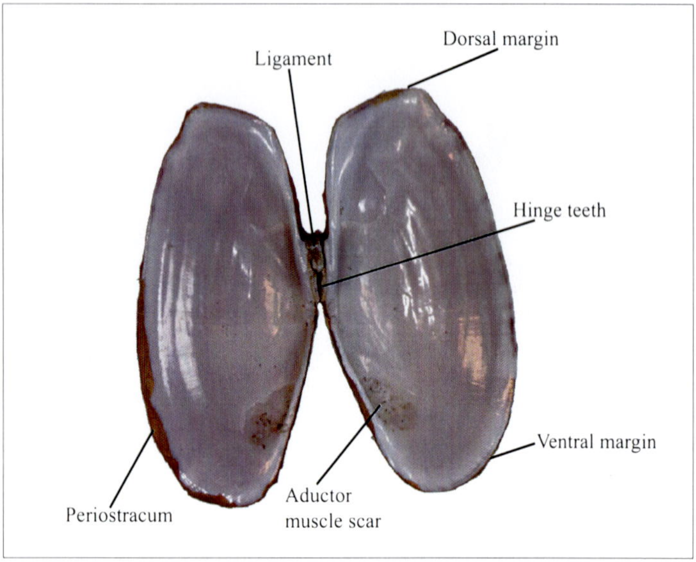
Ligament
Dorsal margin
Hinge teeth
Ventral margin
Periostracum
Aductor
muscle scar

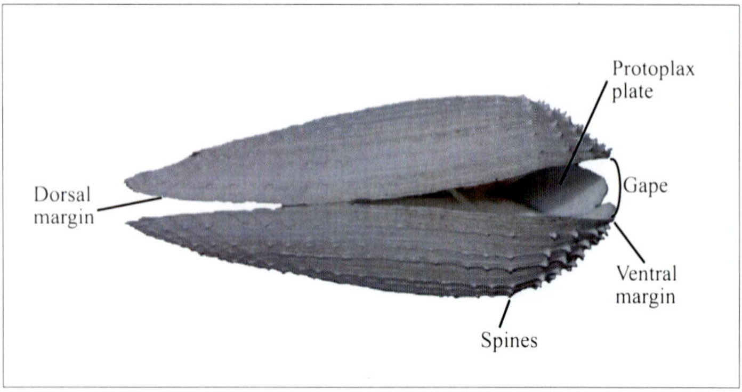
Protoplax
plate
Dorsal
margin
Gape
Ventral
margin
Spines

Microshells

There are more tiny shells than big ones. Below is a sample from weed washings. Usually one or two species predominate in any sample. Different host plants harbour different communities. Most of these are *Barleeia unifasciata* but there are also a few *Rissoa*.

From weed washings, five specieas of Rissoids and a Tricolia (centre) to 6mm

Sample from Cornish crab boat. Most of this batch is sub-adult. The larger shells did not lodge on the strakes!

Calliostoma, Jujubimus and two Trivia

Dredge Options

Diagram 1: As designed and used by West African locals to salvage spilled anthracite or for *Strombus latus*. The original design is towed behind a small boat with two rowers and a sorter. The stern has a built in sorting tray. A smaller but heavier version can be towed on a steel cable by a small trawler. The steel cable takes it down. This is the **BEST** shape and fills quickly taking only the top few inches of the seabed.

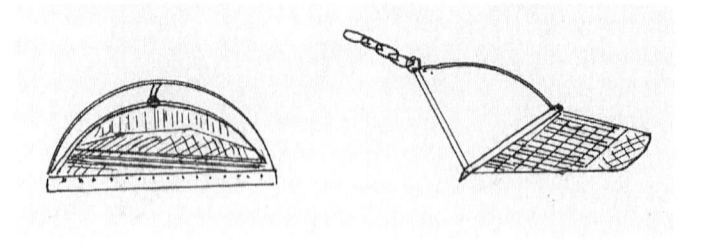

Diagram 2: Naturalist's Dredge. A design recommended in many reference works. This is more difficult to keep to the bottom without snagging. It works better on a level bottom, at a slow drift, than if under power.

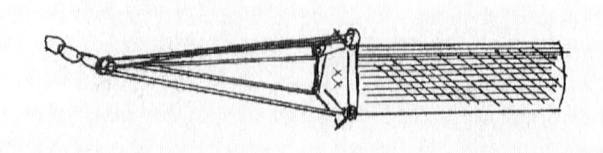

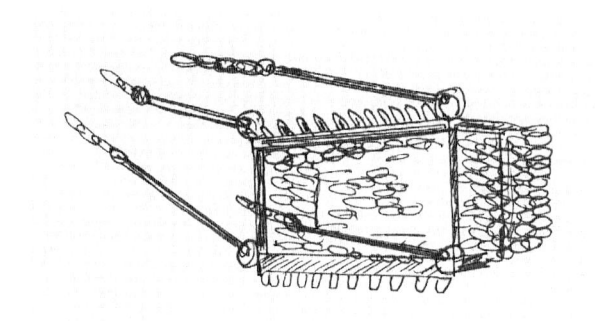

Diagram 3: Commercial Oyster or Scallop Dredge. These are built for use over rough bottoms. They are massively heavy and helped down by massive steel beams. The bag is often steel link so as not to tear out on rocks. The commercial dredgers frequently use these in multiple "gangs" which really chew up the sea bed.

Over mud, an iron bucket on a rope should get you a sample!

Never let the dredge rope go slack. If it gets round the propeller shaft and the propeller is not lost, someone has to dive under the boat and cut it loose. That someone could be you!

Sea Areas

Sea Atlas Areas
Not all Sea Areas fell within the original UK NCC survey as some were outside their geographic remit.
Those covered were:

1.	Shetland	24.	Liverpool Bay
2.	Sutherland	25.	Solway
3.	Orkney	26.	Isle of Man
4.	Viking (West)	27.	Dublin
5.	Morey Firth	28.	Belfast
6.	Aberdeen	29.	Clyde and Argyle
7.	Firth of Forth	29a.	Antrim
8.	North Sea	30.	Minch
9.	Northumberland	31.	Lewis
10.	Dogger	32.	Uist
11.	Yorkshire	33.	North Donegal
12.	Wash	34.	Donegal Bay
13.	Thames	35.	Mayo
14.	East Channel	36.	Galway Bay
15.	Wight	37.	Fastnet
16.	Portland	38.	Cork
17.	Channel Isles	39.	Nymphe Bank
18.	Plymouth	40.	Labadie
19.	Scilly Isles	44.	Rockall
20.	North Cornwall	48.	Faeroes
21.	Bristol Channel		
22.	Cardigan Bay		
23.	Anglesey		

The map was charted by the Conchological Society with Denis R Seaward as Editor.

Shell Collecting Made Simple

Sea Areas Map

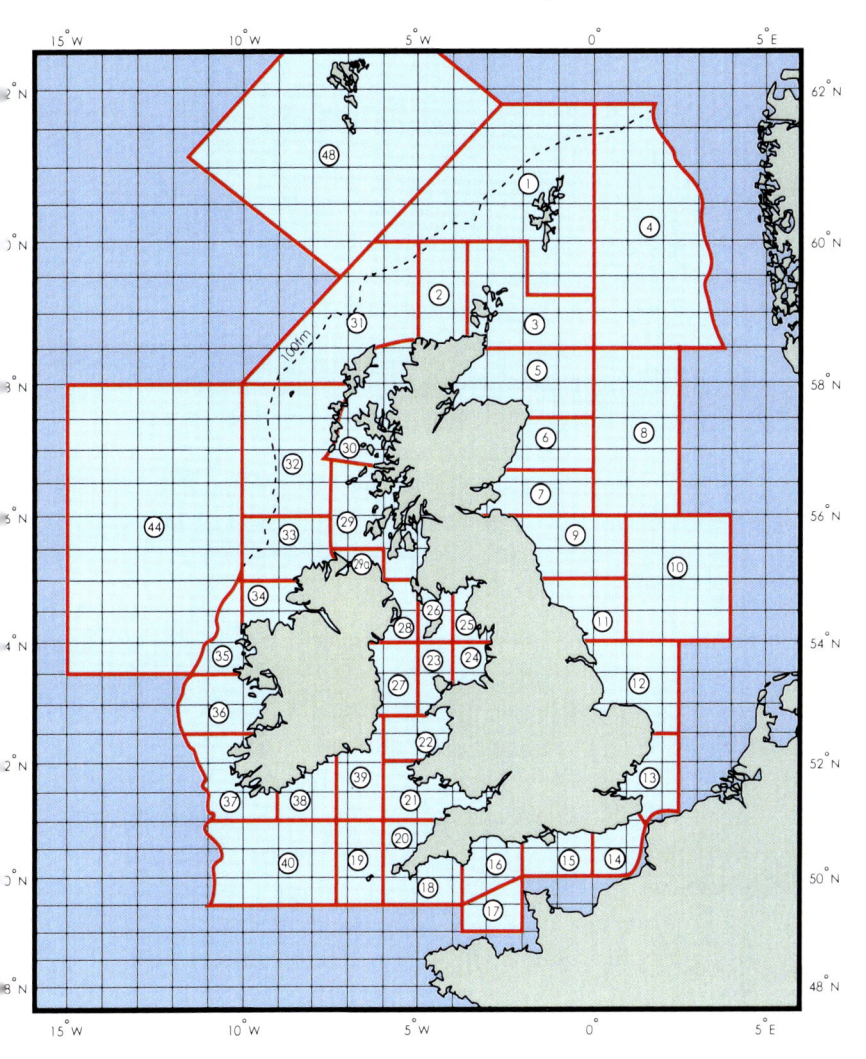

This is a reproduction of the original Sea Area Map for use by the Nature Conservancy Council and the Conchological Society. A ten square kilometer system is now current.

Information

The Conchological Society of Great Britain and Ireland

Founded in 1876, this is one of the oldest societies devoted to the study of molluscs. It normally meets on the second Saturday of the month at the Natural History Museum in London. Their traditional newsletter has recently developed into a glossy colour magazine. Scientific papers are published in their Journal of Conchology. There are also field meetings, study groups and survey activities.
Email: membership @ conchsoc.org
**Honorary membership Secretary: Mike Weideli,
35 Bartelemy Road, Newbury, Berks., RG14 6LD**

The British Shell Collectors' Club

Formally founded in 1977 but informally active earlier, this club addresses the interests of those focussed on the shelled molluscs rather than the full spectrum of Conchology. Two major events, usually an exhibition and a convention, are held each year in the London area. There are also regionally organised activities. The major events are attended by international dealers. There is a bi-annual newsletter called "Palidula". For the full picture see the website which carries a lot of supplementary data: britishshellclub.org.uk
Honorary Secretary: Mrs D Howlett, 6 New Inn Hill, Rockland St Mary, Norwich, Norfolk NR14 7HP

The Malacological Society of London

An organisation to promote education and research into the subject of the Mollusca, it publishes the Journal of Molluscan Studies and the News Bulletin.

This society is best appreciated by those with a real scientific background.

For the full programme see their website:
sunderland.ac.org .

Honorary Secretary: R Cook, PhD, School of Life Sciences, Kingston University, Penryhn Road, Kingston upon Thames, KT1 2EE

A series of European and Worldwide organisations can be accessed via links from the above websites.

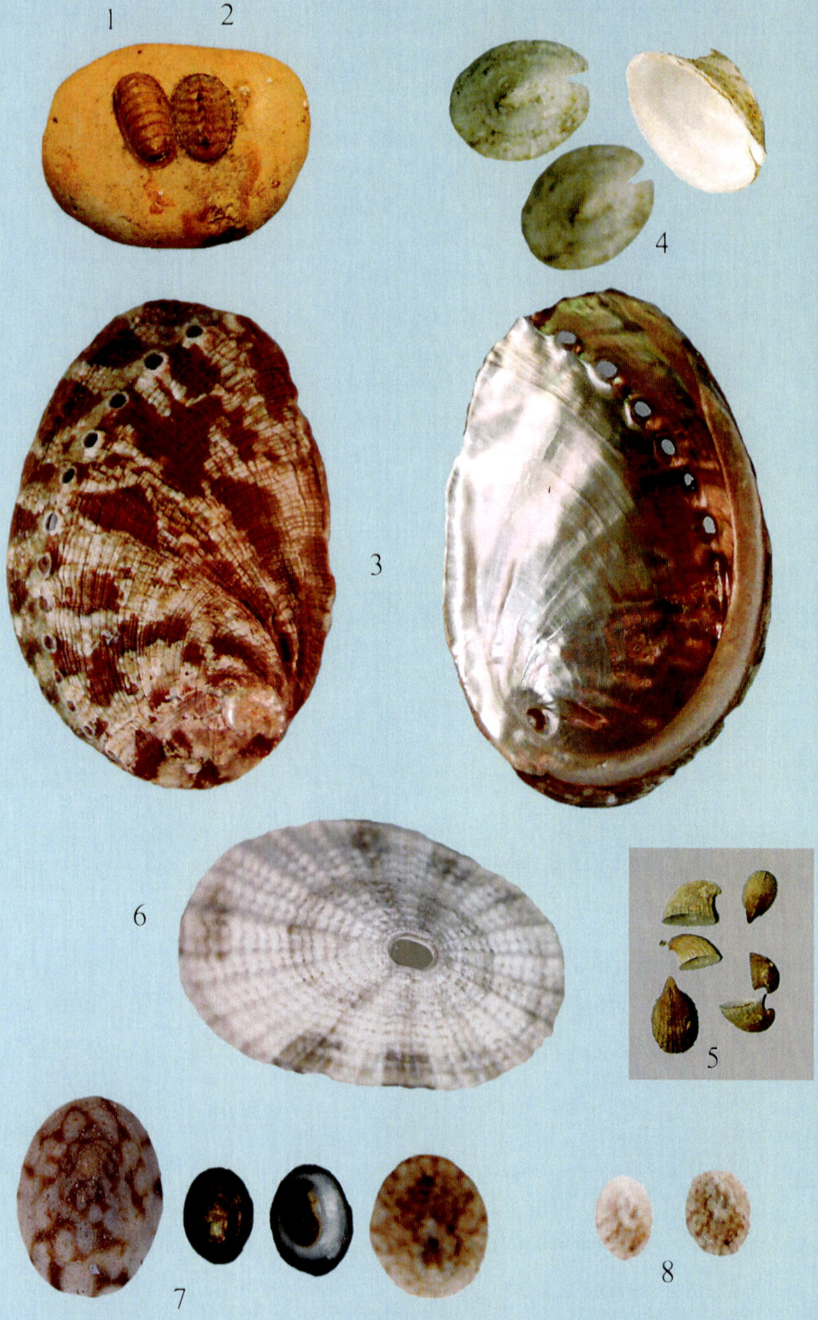
1
2
4
3
6
5
7
8

Shell Collecting Made Simple

1 *Leptochiton asellus* (Gmelin, 1791) Coat of Mail Shells or Chitons
2 *Leptochiton cinereus* (Linne, 1761) Coat of Mail Shells or Chitons
3 *Haliotis tuberculata* Linne, 1758 Ormer or Abalone
4 *Emarginula crassa* J. Sowerby, 1813 Slit Limpet
5 *Emarginula rosea* Bell, 1824 Slit Limpet
6 *Diodora graeca* (Linne, 1758) Keyhole Limpet
7 *Tectura testudinalis* (Muller, 1776) Tortoiseshell Limpet
8 *Tectura virginea* (Muller, 1776)

Chiton shells normally consist of 8 plates linked by a leathery girdle

1 *Leptochiton asellus* to about 12mm	This is the slimmer of our Chitons, which can live inter-tidally, and it requires darkness to prosper. It prefers the lower layers of stones in moving water.
2 *Leptochiton cinereus* to about 14mm	This is the Chiton you are most likely to find under smooth stones, inter-tidal or shallow.

Ormer are large perforated limpets expanding in a flattened spiral. New ventilation holes are constructed and older ones filled in as the animal grows. They are a popular food item but require hammering to make edible.

3 *Haliotis tuberculata* to about 160mm	Although you will only find these on Channel Island beaches, large numbers have been brought to the mainland as ornaments and are easy to obtain.

Slit Limpets live on the under side of rounded stones in moving water. The slit from which they take their name is on the leading edge of a curved cone.

4 *Emarginula crassa* to about 18mm	Northern examples tend to be largest. It has a solid shell with wide aperture appearing flattened.
5 *Emarginula rosea* to about 10mm	Tall and narrow with a pronounced curve, these are locally common as dead shells.

Keyhole Limpets have single characteristic vent holes and are sub-littoral.

6 *Diodora graeca* to about 24mm	These live on stones offshore and wash in dead.

The Tortoiseshell Limpet and its smaller relatives live on or under large rounded stones, usually in shallows.

7 *Tectura testudinalis* to about 34mm usually smaller	A larger, intensely coloured shell, locally common.
8 *Tectura virginea* to about 12mm, usually smaller	Smaller, translucent shells, opaque when dead.

9

10

11

12

9 *Patella depressa*   Pennant, 1777 Lower shore or intermediate Limpet
10 *Patella ulyssiponensis* Gmelin,1791
11 *Patella vulgata*   Linne, 1758   Common Limpet
12 Helcion pellucidum   (Linne,1758)   Blue Rayed Limpet

Limpets live attached to rock, rasping an area clean of vegetation and stopping the settlement of Barnacles in the area where they live. If possible they return to the same point of attachment where their shell exactly fits the rock surface.

9 *Patella depressa*
   to about 45mm

This limpet prefers the lower intertidal zone as it is not as hardy as the Common Limpet. It has a dark grey coloured foot and embeds deeply in soft rock when at rest.

10 *Patella ulyssiponensis*
   to about 80mm

Normally found sub-tidally or in rock pools, this limpet is often washed ashore as a dead shell. It will often appear as a tuft of weed in an otherwise clear area (it has eaten all the other weed!). It has a cream coloured foot. This is potentially the largest of our limpets. In a lot of literature it is referred to as "*Patella aspera*" but revision of taxonomy has shown this name to be a junior synonym and it should not be used.

11 *Patella vulgata*
   to about 65mm

This is a truly common limpet and the only one tough enough to survive on the rocks of the upper shore. The animal is greenish grey or a pale mustard colour. They are sold in some French fish markets though they must be incredibly tough.

Blue Rayed limpets live on the larger kelps rather than rock and can be very thin and delicate.

12 *Helcion pellucidum*
   to about 22mm

Our Blue Rayed limpet lives on Oar Weed or in its root cavities. The typical version lives in the open on the flat surfaces, but if the animal has developed inside the hollow root cavity, a solid, flattened colourless shell is grown.

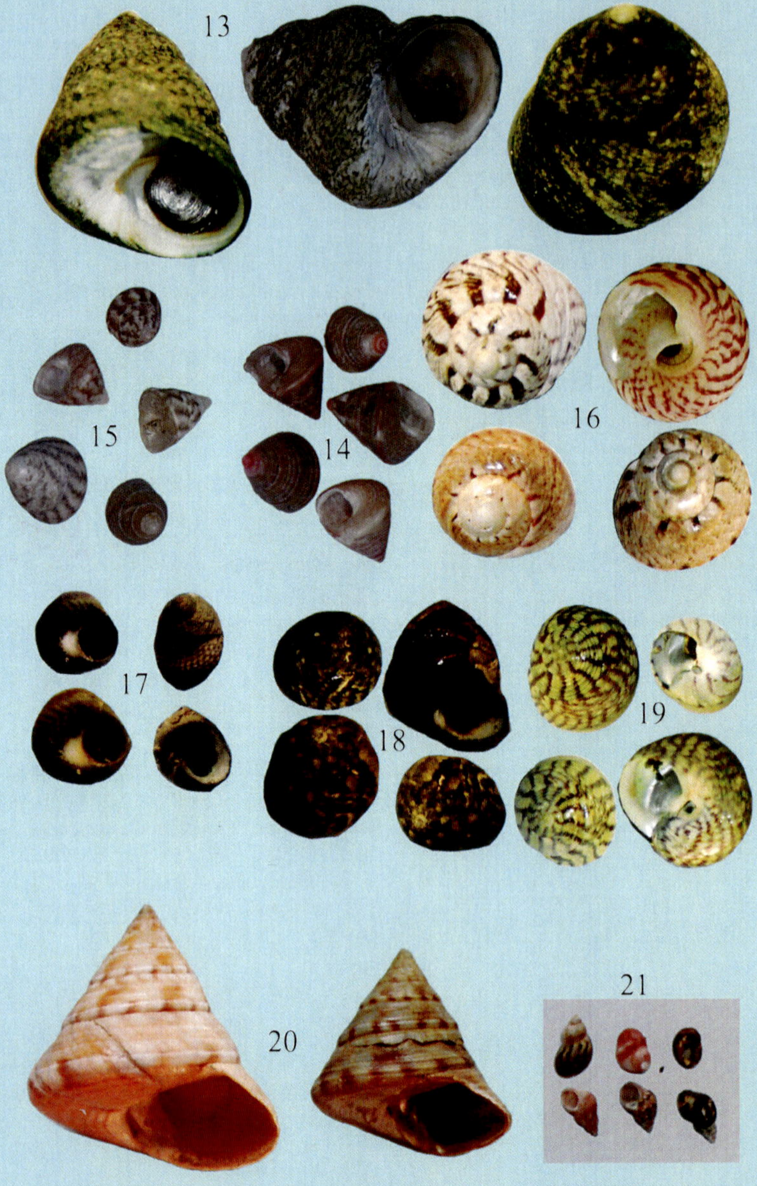
13
15
14
16
17
18
19
20
21

13 *Osilinus lineatus*	(da Costa, 1778)	Top Shells
14 *Jujubinus exasperatus*	(Pennant, 1777)	Top Shells
15 *Jujubinus striatus*	(Linne, 1758)	Top Shells
16 *Gibbula magus*	(Linne, 1758)	Top Shells
17 *Gibbula cineraria*	(Linne, 1758)	Grey Top
18 *Gibbula pennanti*	(Philippi, 1846)	Top shells
19 *Gibbula umbilicalis*	(Muller, 1776)`	Top Shells
20 *Calliostoma zizyphinum*	(Linne, 1758)	Painted Top
21 *Tricolia pullus*	(Linne, 1758)	Pheasant Shells

Top Shells, or Trochids are often found in very large numbers in any suitable habitat. All are vegetarian and most of the species you will find live in shallow water or are intertidal.

13 *Osilinus lineatus*
to about 45mm

This is intertidal but cannot cope with frost. Severe weather results in local extinction and it may take years to recover.

14 *Jujubinus exasperatus*
to about 10mm

Frequent dead in the drift line, these normally live in association with *Zostera* sea grass.

15 *Jujubinus striatus*
to about 10mm

These are less colourful and more symmetrical than exasperatus.

16 *Gibbula magus*
to about 50mm

A solid shell, colourful if Southern but white if Northern, it sometimes washes ashore alive.

17 *Gibbula cineraria*
to about 14mm

The Grey Top lives from the middle intertidal zone on stones and weed. Often abundant!

18 *Gibbula pennanti*
to about 14mm

Southern distribution, it lives in weed, lower inter-tidal zone. It has no umbilicus.

19 *Gibbula umbilicalis*
to about 18mm

In weed, middle to lower intertidal zone and shallows.

20 *Calliostoma zizyphinum*
to 38mm usually smaller

Dead shells frequently wash ashore. Colourful if fresh. Normally sub littoral.

21 *Tricolia pullus*
to about 7mm

Small, brightly coloured shells, common dead in drift lines, they have a ceramic like white operculum. The animal though small is very colourful, usually bright green with white or red marks. These can be found by weed washing in shallows

22

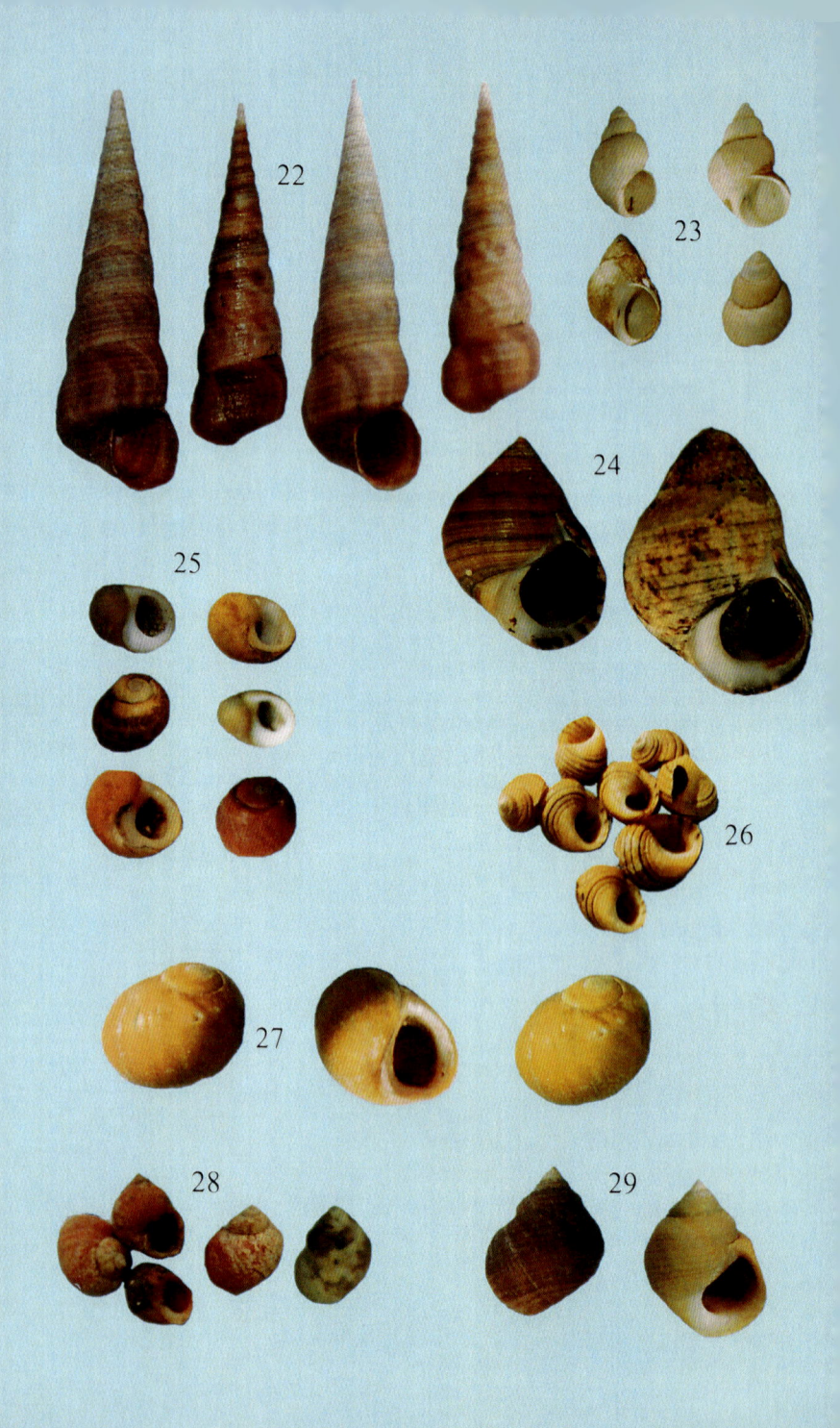

23

24

25

26

27

28

29

22 *Turitella communis*   Risso, 1826   Turret Shells
23 *Lacuna crassior*   (Montagu, 1803)   Thick Lacuna
24 *Littorina littorea*   (Linne, 1758)   Common Winkle
25 *Littorina mariae*   Sacchi & Rastelli, 1966
26 *Littorina nigrolineata* J E Gray, 1839
27 *Littorina obtusata*   (Linne, 1758)   Flat Winkle
28 *Littorina rudis*   (Maton, 1797)
29 *Littorina saxatilis*   (Olivi, 1792)   Rough Periwinkle

Turitella usually live offshore on mud or sand substrates but frequently wash ashore in rough weather, sometimes in large numbers.

22 *Turitella communis* to about 60mm	This turns up in beach drift in modest numbers, it is abundant and widely distributed. They damage easily but perseverance should produce respectable dead specimens.

Lacuna usually wash ashore dead or can be found in weed in shallows. Most are pale coloured and small.

23 *Lacuna crassior* to about 12mm	These are commonest on our Eastern coasts where they wash in with grey weed from the off shore clay beds.

Littorina are incredibly abundant in a range of intertidal habitats. Illustrated are the most obvious of our species. A number of others are adapted to different habitats.

24 *Littorina littorea* to about 32mm	Most specimens are dark brown. This species lives on rocks and is eaten in large numbers.
25 *Littorina mariae* to about 12mm	A small, flattish shell, normally yellow, it prefers sheltered areas on brown or green seaweed.
26 *Littorina nigrolineata* to about 10mm	These live on intertidal granite boulders in the surf. They are viviparous.
27 *Littorina obtusata* to about 17mm	A tough solid species living on bladder wrack. It can be brown or yellow. It is normally much larger than *L. mariae*.
28 *Littorina rudis* to about 20mm	This us usually an estuarine species, sometimes large but taller and slimmer than the others.
29 *Littorina saxatilis* to about 24mm	They have considerable range in size and colour. They colonise areas of rock near the top of the tide. These are not often eaten as they are viviparous and thus seem gritty when chewed.

30

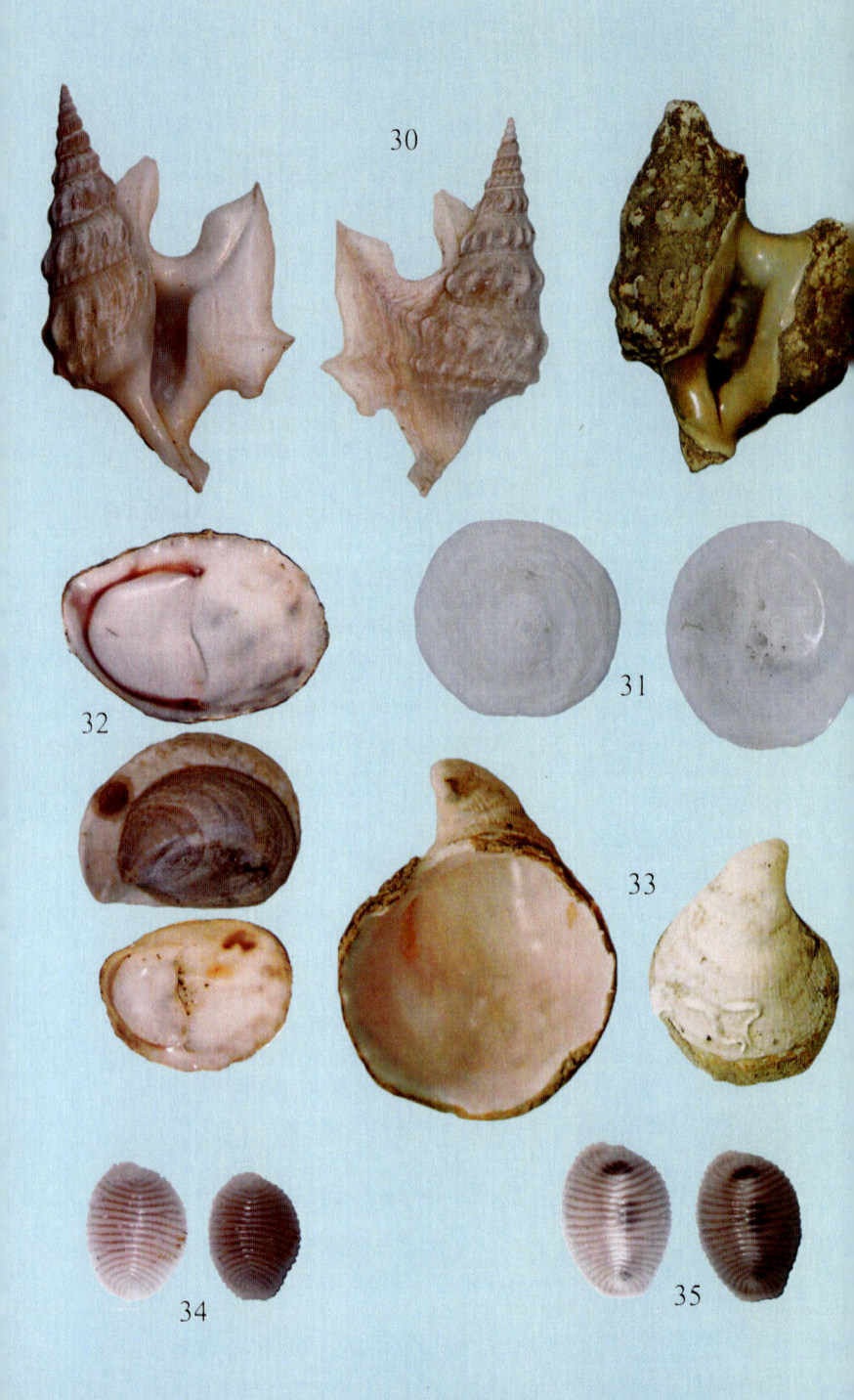

32

31

33

34

35

30 *Aporrhais pespelicani*	(Linne, 1758)	Pelican's Foot
31 *Calyptraea chinensis*	(Linne, 1758)	Chinaman's Hat
32 *Crepidula fornicata*	(Linne, 1758)	Slipper Limpet
33 *Capulus ungaricus*	(Linne, 1758)	Hungarian Cap
34 *Trivia arctica*	(Pultney, 1799)	sometimes referred to as "Cowries"
35 *Trivia monacha*	(Linne, 1758)	but they are not true Cowries!

Aporrhais are our nearest equivalent to the large *Strombus* "Conches" of tropical waters. Our species are detritus feeders.

30 *Aporrhais pespelicani* to about 48mm	These are most likely to be found as dumped cleanings from fishing boats though they do wash ashore in storms. Older examples are thick, heavy and lack elegance.

Calyptraea are limpet like filter feeders but have an internal spiral shelf.

31 *Calyptraea chinensis* to about 20mm	These are common in drift lines, sometimes inside dead shells. A few can be found in shallow water on smooth stones. Two forms exist; one smooth and one stippled.
32 *Crepidula fornicata* to about 62mm	Distribution is uneven but these can be found dead and alive in the drift line in interlocking series, changing sex as they grow. The most mature are in their female phase.

Capulus are widely distributed but sublittoral ciliary feeders that associate with other species, which inadvertently draw food into their reach.

33 *Capulus ungaricus* to about 40mm	While these may wash ashore, your best prospect of getting a live specimen is probably from scallop cleanings.

Trivia are technically carnivorous and are often found in shallow water in association with compound sea-squirts.

34 *Trivia arctica* to about 12mm, often smaller	At one time it was said that our two species of *Trivia* were only colour variants but examination of the mantle demonstrates clear differences. There are no dorsal spots. Dead shells tend to look pink rather than beige.
35 *Trivia monacha* to about 26mm. An exceptional specimen in the NHM.	Although adult T.monacha have spotted dorsums, the juveniles are white. Most deeper water specimens are this species.

36

37

38

39

40

41

Shell Collecting Made Simple

36 *Velutina velutina* (Muller, 1776) Smooth Lamellaria
37 *Polinices catena* (da Costa, 1778) Necklace Shells, Natica or Moon
38 *Polinices fuscus* (Blainville, 1825) Snails
39 *Polinices polianus* (delle Chiage, 1826)
40 *Epitonium clathrus* (Linne, 1758) Wentletraps
41 *Epitonium turtonis* (Turton, 1819)

Velutina are fragile shells, purple or tan in colour, which have a velvety periostracum when fresh.

36 *Velutina velutina* to about 24mm	These shells are normally sublittoral but wash ashore, usually without their periostracum.

Necklace shells drill holes in their prey. These holes have bevelled edges and are easily recognised. While alive and mobile, the shell is covered by its mantle as it ploughs through the sand in search of bivalves. The name Necklace Shell comes from its egg case's strong resemblance to an African necklace. These are formed from sand gummed into shape with mucus.

37 *Polinices catena* to about 24mm	This is the largest of the local *Polinices*. It has muted spiral patterns on its early whorls but adults may be plain. They move inshore in breeding season.
38 *Polinices fuscus* to about 16mm	Normally a sublittoral species which washed ashore dead. They have a red-brown periostracum and a more pronounced spire.
39 *Polinices polianus* to about 14mm	These used to be known as "*Natica alderi*" in error. All *Polinices* have plain horny opercula whereas Naticids have thicker, shell like opercula. A fresh shell is often attractively marked with bands of chevrons. Offshore shells are pale.

Wentletraps take their common name from the Dutch for staircase. This name originated with the formerly rare Precious Wentletrap. They usually feed on sea anemones but this may not always be the case as I have found them in places where there were no anemones.

40 *Epitonium clathrus* to about 44mm	While this species is not uncommon as a dead shell, live ones are scarce. I have found them in shallow water only in April.
41 *Epitonium turtonis* to about 58mm	This is usually a deeper water shell washing ashore in small numbers from time to time. It seems to be a variable species but further study may result in separate populations being recognised.

42

43

44

45

46

42 *Ocenebra erinacea* (Linne, 1758)   Sting Winkle
43 *Ocenebra aciculata* (Lamarck, 1822)
44 *Urosalpinx cinerea* (Say, 1822)   Oyster Drill
45 *Nucella lapillus* (Linne, 1758)   Dog Whelk
46 *Buccinum undatum* (Linne, 1758)   Whelk

Ocenebra are carnivores preying on other molluscs or barnacles.

42 *Ocenebra erinacea* to about 42mm	These normally live in fairly shallow water and are common as dead shells. The animal is white with a tan operculum.
43 *Ocenebra aciculata* about 14mm	This is mainly a Southern species. The Latin name was given because the animal is a bright coral red.

Urosalpinx are native to America but naturalised here after being imported with cultivated oysters.

44 *Urosalpinx cinerea* to about 24mm	In England I have only found this as dead shells in Essex and Kent. Live specimens in Florida were seen in quite shallow water in tidal rivers.

Nucella are an abundant predator associated with barnacle or mussel covered rocks in the intertidal zone but live specimens from crab pots prove they can also live deeper. Those from deep water tide races show serious wear.

45 *Nucella lapillus* to about 54mm	There are many locally distinct populations, variable in size and colour. White shells with a tinge of violet to the aperture are the most common though larger, banded forms exist. These are edible but VERY tough to chew.

These are the Whelks normally sold in European fishmongers and are consumed in huge numbers. Most are trapped offshore but they can also be found alive at Spring tide low water.

46 *Buccinum undatum* to about 140mm	These are primarily scavengers taken by baited traps and their empty shells are favourites with hermit crabs. A small number of them are "sinistral" i.e. the spiral is reversed. This is believed to be a local genetic aberration.

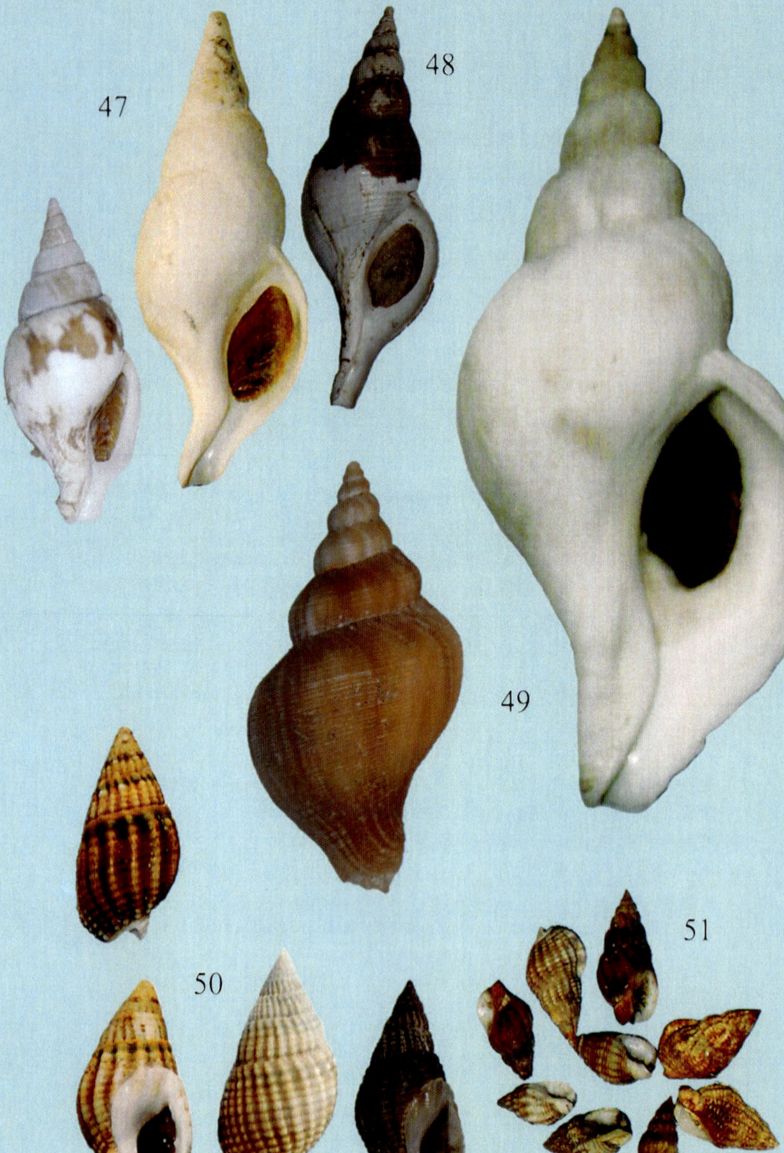
47
48
49
50
51

47 *Colus gracilis*   (da Costa, 1778)   Spindle Whelk
48 *Colus islandica* (Mohr, 1822)
49 *Neptunea antiqua* (Linne, 1758)   Neptune Shell
50 *Hinia reticulata* (Linne, 1758)   Netted Whelk
51 *Hinia incrassata* (Strom, 1768)

Colus are elegant deep water snails, which sometimes come in with commercial whelk catches or are walked ashore by hermit crabs. *Colus* shells are white but the living animals are usually bright red.

47 *Colus gracilis*
   to about 70mm
Normally stockier than islandica, its siphonal canal is more curved. Fresh specimens have a thin brownish periostracum.

48 *Colus islandica*
   to about 110mm
This is mainly a Northern species. It is much larger and has a longer straighter siphonal canal. The periostracum tends to golden rather than brown shades.

Neptunea are circum polar boreal species, more abundant in the North, but some very deep water species extend round the Iberian Peninsula and at least one lives in the Gulf of Mexico.

49 *Neptunea antiqua*
   to about 220mm
But usually smaller there are two colour forms; the smaller brown version seems to prefer hard clay substrates in moderately deep water but are commonly beached. The large white shells come from well offshore. Big examples, which are brown and have flared apertures, do exist but I am not sure where they originate. Sinistral shells are often found in East Anglian beach drift but these are locally extinct crag fossils, which have washed out of the iron sand cliffs.

Hinia were widely called *Nassarius* prior to taxonomic revision. They are abundant shallow water scavengers.

50 *Hinia reticulata*
   to about 35mm
This species favours level sandy or muddy bottoms where it will be attracted to any available carrion. They leave trails in the sand or mud.

51 *Hinia incrassata*
   to about 15mm
These attractive small shells have a huge geographic range. They prefer areas of intertidal rock and weed holdfasts.

52

53

55

54

56

57

58

52 *Oenopota turricula*	(Montagu, 1803)	Turret Shell
53 *Comarmondia gracilis*	(Montagu, 1803)	
54 *Haminoea hydatis*	(Linne, 1758)	Bubble Shell
55 *Acteon tornatilis*	(Linne, 1758)	Banded Acteon
56 *Scaphander lignarius*	(Linne, 1758	Canoe Bubble
57 *Akera bullata*	Muller, 1776	
58 *Antalis entalis*	(Linne, 1758)	Tooth Shell

Turrids usually live in sand covering a hard substrate as they hunt worms and these are easier to find if they cannot burrow deep. This family can be recognised by the "turrid notch" where the lip joins the shoulder.

52 *Oenopota turricula*
  to about 20mm
While I have found these regularly on Essex beaches and more rarely round Southern England I have never seen a live one. It is thought to be circumpolar.

53 *Comarmondia gracilis*
  to about 30mm
One of our most beautiful shells. Alive, it has bright violet bands (white when dead). It usually lives a little off shore.

Haminoea live in areas of muddy sand from the lower shore down to considerable depth.

54 *Haminoea hydatis*
  to about 24mm
These bubble shells live in sublittoral weed. I have always assumed they were carnivores but this may not be correct.

Acteons are carnivores preying on polychaetes worms from the low intertidal zone and deeper, over a wide distribution.

55 *Acteon tornatilis*
  to about 24mm
  but usually smaller
This normally offshore species comes to shallow water once a year to breed and most of the shells you will find largely are casualties of this migration.

Scaphander live from the lower intertidal zone to considerable depth. They have internal gastric plates for crushing small bivalves. The animal is large.

56 *Scaphander lignarius*
  to about 70mm
These have thin but strong shells with a light brown periostracum. Try fishermen's net cleanings.

Akera are mainly herbivorous and prefer silty bottoms in either shallow bays or deeper water. There are two main forms believed to be conspecific.

57 *Akera bullata*
  to 22mm
Two forms exist, the smaller in astronomical numbers in silty saline lagoons. You may find drifts of dead shells. The larger more mobile form prefers deep black mud.

Tusk shells prefer sublittoral sand but a lot wash ashore. They are symmetrical tubes with a burrowing foot.

58 *Antalis entalis*
  to about 40mm
Robust white shells. They are frequently attacked by crabs and have heavy repair scars if the crab fails to kill and eat them.

59

60

61

62

63

64

65

59 *Nucula nucleus*	(Linne, 1758)	Nut Shell
60 *Arca tetragona*	Poli, 1795	Ark Shell
61 *Striarca lactea*	(Linne, 1758)	White Ark
62 *Glycymeris glycymeris*	(Linne, 1758)	Bittersweet
63 *Mytillus edulis*	Linne, 1758	Mussel
64 *Modiolus adriaticus*	(Lamarck, 1819)	Adriatic Horse Mussel
65 *Modiolus modiolus*	(Linne, 1758)	Horse Mussel

Nucula are small brown shells lined with mother-of pearl. They are frequently found in the drift line as single valves. Paired valves are more difficult to spot.

59 *Nucula nucleus* — The most common of the family, these live
   to about 10mm — in clay, gravel or sand from shallow water down to 100+ metres.

Ark shells usually live attached by byssus threads under or between stones.

60 *Arca tetragona* — More often found as dead shells in the drift
   to about 50mm — line. They usually have a brown and white zigzag pattern. The hinge is long and has many small teeth.

61 *Striarca lactea* — A small white shell usually between
   to about 10mm — shallow water stones. Most have a light brown periostracum.

Bittersweets live from the shallows down to quite deep water in sand or gravel. They are eaten on the continent, sold under the name of "Almondes."

62 *Glycymeris glycymeris* — An attractively marked, heavy shell with
   to about 80mm — crenulated edges and strong hinge teeth.

Mussels are probably the most popular of all edible mollusca and are farmed on a vast scale in France and Spain.

63 *Mytilus edulis* — These live in rocks from mid tide down.
   to about 90mm — Commercial beds are sometimes cultivated
   but usually smaller — on rope frames. Most are blue-black though some populations are black with blue rays.

64 *Modiolus adriaticus* — These have a Southern distribution. They
   to about 35mm — may be golden brown or yellow. Red variants exist in African populations.

65 *Modiolus modiolus* — Older examples may be encased in coralline
   to about 140mm — algae and be very large. Huge beds exist on otherwise muddy bottoms, creating their own hard substrate. Their byssus holdfasts may include interesting deep-water shells.

67

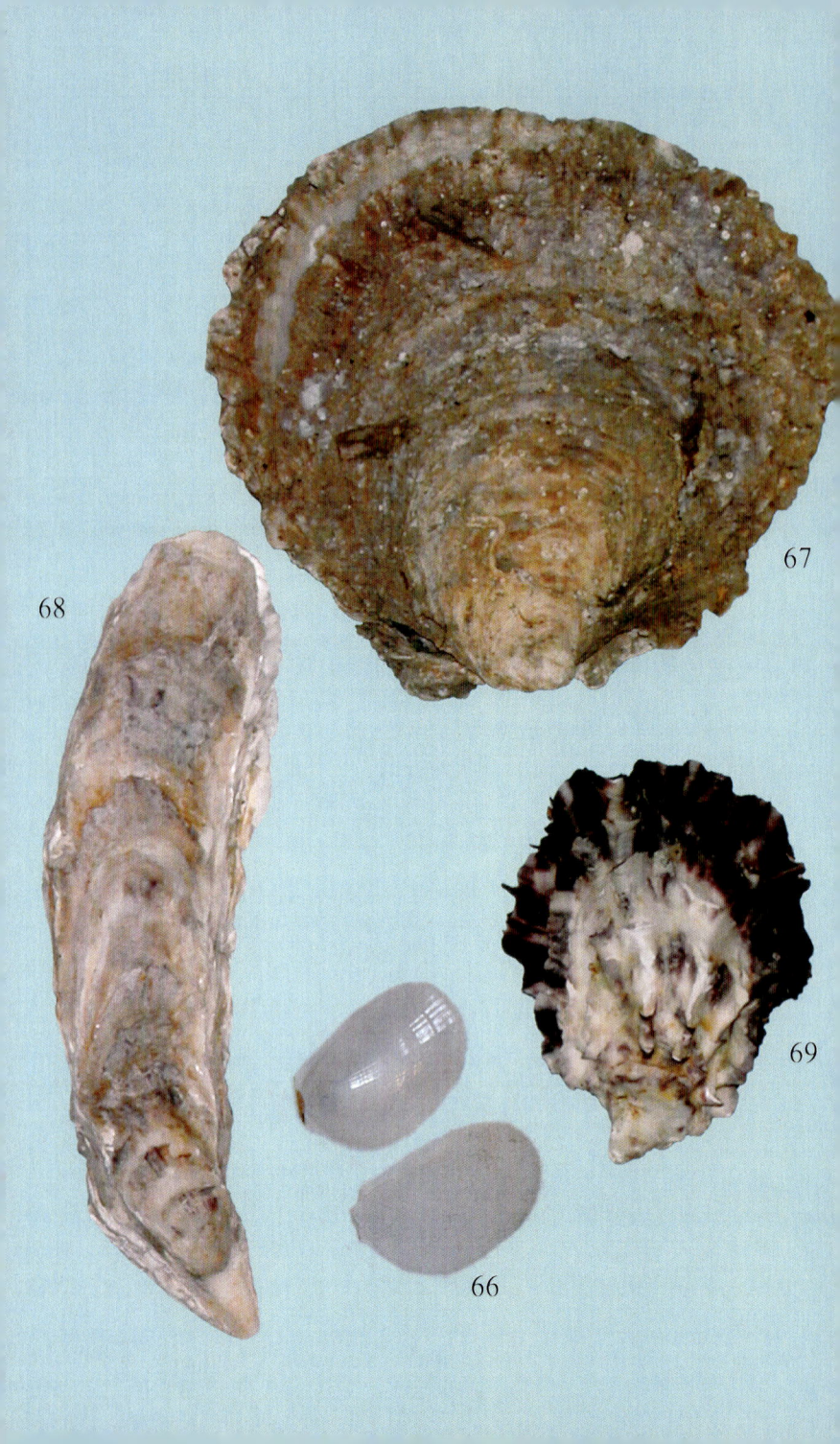

68

69

66

66 *Limaria hians*   (Gmelin, 1791)   File Shell
67 *Ostrea edulis*   Linne, 1758   Native Oyster
68 *Crasostrea gigas* (Thunberg, 1793)   Giant Oyster
69 *Crasostrea virginica* Linne, 1758   Virginian Oyster

Limaria hide under sublittoral stones but can swim using red or orange tentacles. They are normally brilliantly white under a thin brown periostracum.

66 *Limaria hians*   These are not easy to collect alive but the
  to about 26mm   delicate white shells are not uncommon in
                             beach drift.

Oysters have always been a popular delicacy, often eaten raw and are widely cultivated because demand has outstripped the supply. Young of several normally foreign species have been imported to Europe to replenish dwindling local stocks.

67 *Ostrea edulis*   The ideal habitat is a bay or estuary with
  to about 150mm   continuous current and a hard substrate for
                             the settling of spat (juvenile oysters).
                             Millions of eggs are produced but as they
                             are filter feeders, there is large scale
                             cannibalism.

68 *Crasostrea gigas*   This primarily Southern species can grow
  to about 250mm   very large if permitted to survive. Those
                             you see in supermarkets are very young.
                             Purists consider the flavour a little inferior
                             to that of the Native Oyster.

69 *Crasostrea virginica*   This American species has been imported
  to about 110mm   to traditional areas of Oyster cultivation
                             because it matures faster than our own.
                             Some specimens are decorated with ornate
                             purple scales.

72

70

71

73

75

74

70 *Chlamys distorta* (da Costa, 1778)
71 *Chlamys varia* (Linne, 1758)
72 *Pecten maximus* (Linne, 1758) Great Scallop or
more usually just Scallop
73 *Aequipecten opercularis* (Linne, 1758) Queen Scallop
74 *Palliolum tigerinum* (Muller, 1776) Tiger Scallop
75 *Pseudamussium*
septemradiatum (Muller, 1776)

Scallops are usually able to swim using muscle contractions to jet water from their mantle. Starfish will eat Scallops and their presence triggers a lot of activity. While many live in deeper water, several species can be found in shallows or attached by byssus under stones.

70 *Chlamys distorta*
to about 60mm
These exist both as attached or free swimming forms and the latter was at one time given the name "multistriata". The lower valve is typically firmly attached to rock so only the upper valve washes ashore.

71 *Chlamys varia*
to about 70mm
Their size is usually smaller in our waters. As the name suggests, many colours can be found. Most of those I have found personally were dark brown and attached under stones in moving water at low tide.

72 *Pecten maximus*
to about 170mm
A large shell commercially fished, most specimens are dark brown but purple, white or patterned examples can be found. Living shells wash ashore if weed or large kelp has anchored on their shells.

73 *Aequipecten opercularis*
to about 70mm
The most attractive colours are normally from deeper waters but the normal pink to brown shells are most likely to turn up in the drift line. They are sometimes trawled commercially.

74 *Palliolum tigerinum*
to about 26mm
Very variable and attractive small shells but usually only found as single valves on beaches, these are sometimes recovered in large numbers from cods' stomachs. The best specimens seem to come from the Irish Sea. Some Northern examples have thicker shells with pronounced ribbing.

75 *Pseudamussium*
septemradiatum
to about 50mm
These are most likely to be recovered from net cleanings as they are usually taken in deeper water. The strength of the ribbing is variable.

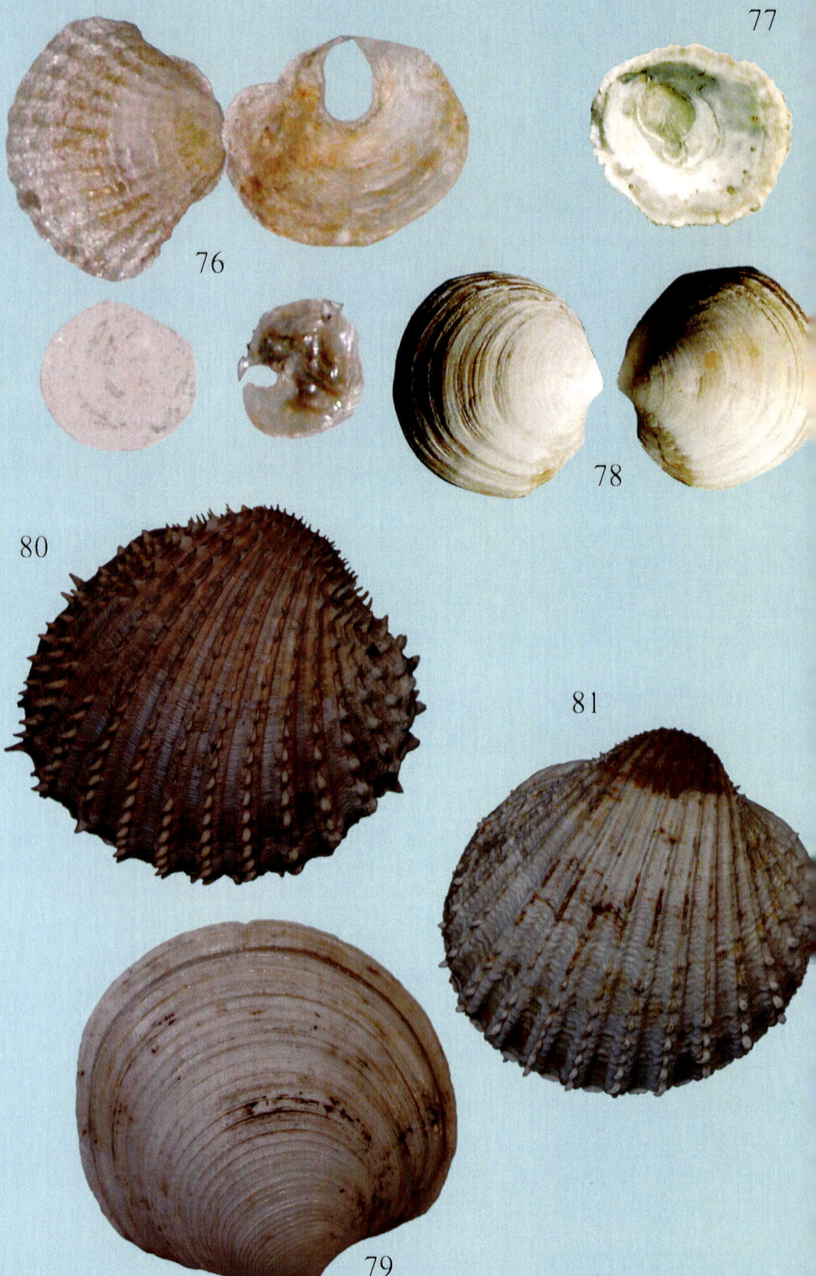
77
76
78
80
81
79

76 *Anomia ephippium*   Linne, 1758   Saddle Oyster or Jingle Shell
77 *Heteranomia squamula* (Linne, 1758)
78 *Loripes lucinalis*   (Lamarck, 1818)   Lucines
79 *Lucinoma borealis*   (Linne, 1758)
80 *Acanthocardia aculeata* (Linne, 1758)   Spiny Cockle
81 *Acanthocardia echinata* (Linne, 1758)   Prickly Cockle

Saddle Oysters attach to stones or other shells, taking on the profile of the attachment. On a Scallop they are corrugated. Inside a gastropod they are concave.

76 *Anomia ephippium* to about 50mm	Thin shells giving a metallic appearance of pearl. Muscle scarring inside the upper shell area is a single blotch.
77 *Heteranomia squamula* to about 40mm	A thicker rougher shell with one large and one smaller muscle scar. They are less common than ephippium.

Lucines are mainly small white burrowers in sand and usually sublittoral but may also be found in saline lagoons.

78 *Loripes lucinalis* to about 20mm	Often found in intertidal, muddy sand and may wash out of bait diggers' operations. They prefer sheltered waters.
79 *Lucinoma borealis* to about 40mm	These seem to live just offshore. Northern and Channel Island specimens grow much larger than the South coast population, which may be genetically distinct.

Cockles are commercially important. Smaller species also exist.

80 *Acanthocardia aculeata* to about 100mm	In its natural habitat the cockle really is spiny but the spines break off while washing in, mainly on the South coast. When intact the spines are long, sharp and curved. It is our largest Cockle but rather fragile.
81 *Acanthocardia echinata* to 60mm	These are widely distributed and adults are more usual offshore. Small juveniles wash ashore in South facing sandy bays. It may be recognised by the saw tooth ridges along each rib of the shell.

82

84

83

85

82 *Acanthocardia tuberculata* (Linne, 1758)   Red Nose Cockle
83 *Laevicardium crassum*   (Gmelin, 1791)   Norwegian Cockle
84 *Cerastoderma edule*   (Linne, 1758)   Cockle
85 *Cerastoderma glaucum*   (Poiret, 1789)

82 *Acanthocardia tuberculata* to 80mm, usually smaller — It takes its English name from its brightly coloured foot. This is a robust shell with coarse blunt sculpture if it has grown in an exposed area but some from sheltered waters develop fine sculpture with peg like spines. British specimens are normally light brown but Southern populations may have albino or chocolate brown shells.

83 *Laevicardium crassum* to 80mm, usually smaller — These are widely distributed and live from just offshore to considerable depths. Our specimens are larger than the average for the species. They have a thin periostracum.

84 *Cerastoderma edule* to 55mm, usually smaller — Astronomically abundant and distributed from the Arctic to Senegal, they prefer clean sandy bays and live from mid tide level to just below low water mark. Many beds are commercially exploited.

85 *Cerastoderma glaucum* to 35mm, usually smaller — This species was at one time known by the name *lamarcki*. It is thinner and the ribs show clearly on the inside of the shell. It can be attractively coloured but is generally smaller than edule. Saline lagoons are the preferred habitat. They are more mobile than *edule* and can climb using the foot to gain purchase, even on glass.

88

86

89

90

87

86 *Mactra stultorum*	(Linne, 1758)	Surf Clams
87 *Spisula solida*	(Linne, 1758)	Trough Shells
88 *Spisula subtruncata*	(da Costa, 1778)	
89 *Lutraria angustior*	(Philippi, 1844)	
90 *Lutraria lutraria*	(Linne, 1758)	Otter Shells

There are two species of *Mactra* in British waters, one very common and one very rare. Both live in clean sand from just below low tide to far off shore.

86 *Mactra stultorum* to 40mm	The name "corallina" was at one time applied to these. Some shells are attractively rayed others, particularly juveniles, are translucent white or grey. Bad weather can wash them ashore by the thousand to die on the beach.
87 *Spisula solida* to 35mm	This is the largest of our *Spisula* and most of the specimens which reach the drift line arrive as dead adults.
88 *Spisula subtruncata* to 17mm	These are smaller and less symmetrical wedge shaped shells which frequently wash ashore alive.

Otter shells can be locally very common though normally less so on normal sea shores. I have seen vast numbers dead on the banks of tidal rivers and divers report huge drifts of dead shells in deep water below the Chesil Bank. While most authors rely on the scars of muscle attachment for identification, this is only necessary for really bad specimens as there are bigger differences of the siphon structures, which are easily seen if the animal is intact.

89 *Lutraria angustior* to 140mm	This is usually a thick, broad shell with dark periostracum. It can be found living in intertidal runoff channels. The siphons are more elegant than those of L. lutraria and the tip is like a coral coloured sea anemone.
90 *Lutraria lutraria* to 130mm	These wash ashore in winter storms. If you arrive before the gulls you will see massive brown and white speckled siphons, longer than the actual shell. Distribution is scattered but it can be very common. The periostracum is thin and greyish.

91

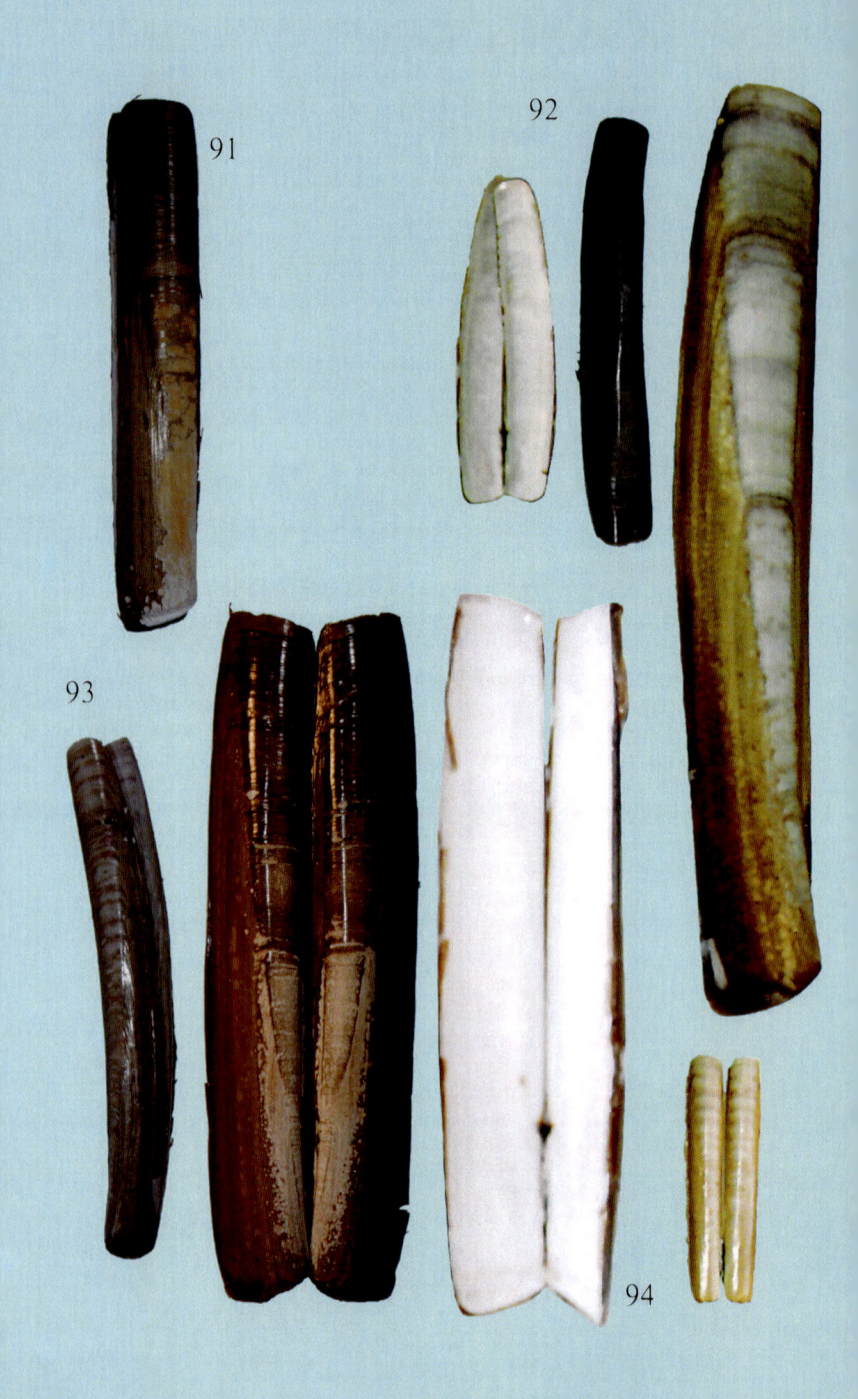

92

93

94

91 *Solen marginatus*   Pultney, 1799   Razor Shells
92 *Ensis arcuatus*   (Jeffreys, 1865)
93 *Ensis ensis*   (Linne, 1758)
94 *Ensis siliqua*   (Linne, 1758)

We have several species of Razor Shells – the name being taken from their resemblance to the traditional cutthroat razor. Some immigrant species are also beginning to establish populations. All live from low in the intertidal zone to considerable depths. The latter is more unusual. Populations are able to migrate ejecting themselves from their burrows at low tide and trapping air bubbles. The shell then floats horizontally then drifts with the current. Air is gradually released till the animal is vertical and neutrally buoyant in mid water. A smaller bubble is then released and the animal drifts over the sea bed testing for suitable sand. When a satisfactory spot is found, more air is released and the foot tunnels vertically into the sand. Of course it can all go desperately wrong. There are mass strandings and you will find stubs of shell sticking up because the sand was not as deep as they hoped it was. Seagulls eat most of them.

91 *Solen marginatus*
    to 140mm

These are straight shells with hinge teeth at the bottom corner. The distinguishing feature is a groove or collar round the lower margin. *Solen* are easiest to find in shallows at low tide. They are sometimes collected by pouring salt down their burrows. The shell comes out to eject the salt. They are eaten in France and Spain. Our cat hunted them in Portland Harbour.

92 *Ensis arcuatus*
    to 150mm

The second largest of our species, they are broad and slightly curved.

93 *Ensis ensis*
    to 110mm

Slim curved shells, widespread but seldom in such numbers as the other species. The periostracum is greenish brown.

94 *Ensis siliqua*
    to 180mm

Strong straight shells, with a periostracum from brown to almost black. The largest of the family in our waters.

95
96
97
99
101
100
102

95 *Angulus squalidus*	(Pultney,1799)	Tellins
96 *Angulus tenuis*	(da Costa, 1778)	
97 *Arcopagia crassa*	(Pennant, 1777)	
98 *Fabulina fabula*	(Gmelin,1791)	
99 *Moerella donacina*	(Linne, 1758)	
100 *Donax variegatus*	(Gmelin, 1791)	Wedge Shells
101 *Donax vittatus*	(da Costa, 1778)	
102 *Macoma balthica*	(Linne,1758)	Baltic Tellin

Tellins are slim attractive shells. They are filter feeders, buried in sand with their siphons extending to the water above. The upper lip has a distortion or twist.

95 Angulus squalidus
to 48mm

This uncommon species has long siphons and buries deep. Most specimens I have found living had lost part of their foot. I believe that wading birds with long bills are responsible. Colours range through cream to orange and pink.

96 Angulus tenuis
to 22mm

These brightly coloured shells are common in most clean sand drift lines.

97 Arcopagia crassa
to 40mm

These are more solid than the other Tellins. They prefer a mix of gravel and sand at very low tide or a little way offshore. Inside they may be pink. Pale yellow examples may be found. Some have pink or red axial rays.

98 Fabulina fabula
to 18mm

Slim shells, white or cream in colour. They can be incredibly abundant in the right conditions. One valve has sculpture of wavy lines.

99 Moerella donacina
to 20mm

A very attractive shell usually found in the drift line rather than alive. Distribution is irregular but extensive. Cream shells with red rays.

100 Donax variegatus
to 32mm

It is the least common of our *Donax*, and distinguishable by its inner lips being smooth rather than serrated.

101 Donax vittatus
to 40mm

Abundant on the right beaches, colours range through yellow brown and violet with brown axial rays.

102 Macoma balthica
to 20mm

This species can tolerate lower salinity than the others. It is super-abundant at the Northern end of its range, less so in the South West. The shells are solid and display a range of pastel colours.

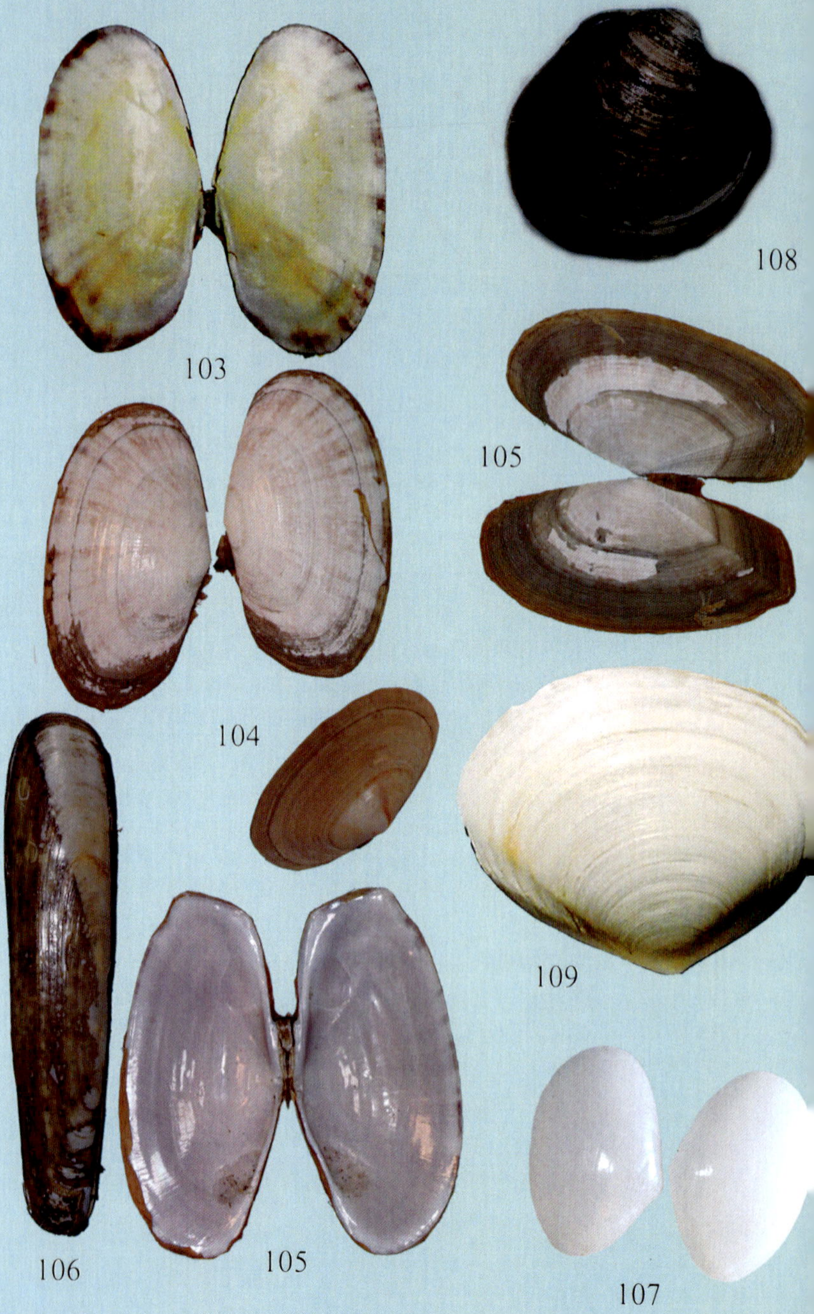
108
103
105
104
109
106
105
107

103 *Gari depressa*	(Pennant, 1777)	Sunset Shell
104 *Gari tellinella*	(Lamarck, 1818)	
105 *Gari fervensis*	(Gmelin, 1791)	
106 *Pharus legumen*	(Linne, 1758)	
107 *Abra alba*	(W. Wood, 1802)	
108 *Arctica islandica*	(Linne, 1767)	Cyprina
109 *Scrobicularia plana*	(da Costa, 1778)	

The Sunset Shells are rayed, often mauve or purple inside, and are shallow burrowers at a 45 degree angle, at extreme low tide level or deeper. These are not as common as most literature suggests but do turn up on beaches over time.

103 *Gari depressa*
to 48mm
An attractive shell, usually only found dead in drift lines or shallows.

104 *Gari tellinella*
to 22mm
Attractive shells in a range of bright pastel shades, they seem to deposit high on the strand line rather than the drift line because of their very light weight.

105 *Gari fervensis*
to 46mm
I have found these in sandy shallows still alive and a few dead ones in the drift line.

Pharus are usually washed ashore dead on open West or South West facing beaches and are locally common though difficult to find alive.

106 *Pharus legumen*
to 76mm
These prefer wide-open, gradually shelving, sandy bays. A central hinge and rounded ends distinguishes them from Ensis.

Abra are thin white shells common on most gently shelving silty sand beaches.

107 *Abra alba*
to 16mm
Translucent white shells from silty sand from low water down. These are frequent both alive and dead in the drift line.

This may be the only surviving species in its genus. It is widely distributed in cold waters and is very slow growing. Big specimens may be more than 200 years old. Americans refer to this shell as the "Quahog". It can be found on beaches but the best specimens are trawled in the Irish Sea.

108 *Arctica islandica*
to 120mm
Large discus shaped shells with black periostracum on a white base. It is said to prefer muddy bottoms.

Some authors place *Scrobicularia* in the same family as *Abra*, which is regarded by some as part of the *Semelidae*. All are white, filter feeders but some of the Southern species of *Scrobicularia* are more readily separable from the *Semelidae*.

109 *Scrobicularia plana*
to 60mm
Preferring soft muddy bottoms, this species has very long siphons for its size. Flowing brackish water seems to produce the highest population densities. The French are now harvesting them for human consumption.

110

111

112

113

114

115

110 *Venus verrucosa*   Linne, 1758
111 *Gouldia minima*   (Montagu, 1803)
112 *Chamalea gallina*   (Linne, 1758)
113 *Clausinella fasciata*   (da Costa, 1778)
114 *Mercenaria mercenaria*   (Linne, 1758)
115 *Timoclea ovata*   (Pennant, 1777)

The Venus Shells are a very large family with populations worldwide. Some of our own species extend across the equator. Species living intertidally in one area may be deep water in others. Some are small in shallow water but twice as large if deeper. This may mean that the deepwater shells are not in an environment where they reach breeding condition and just keep growing.

110 *Venus verrucosa* to about 50mm
: This hardy species can thrive on open coastlines. A gravel substrate is preferred. Those from sheltered water are often smaller. Although sold commercially in France, they do not taste as good as some of their relatives.

111 *Gouldia minima* to 12mm
: Flat symmetrical shells, sometimes white but usually with tented patterns, these grow larger offshore and only small ones reach the drift line.

112 *Chamalea gallina* to 24mm
: Our population was formerly called *C. striatula* but the new perception is that it is not separable from the earlier named Mediterranean population. They wash ashore alive and dead on a regular basis in most sandy shores.

113 *Clausinella fasciata* to 22mm
: A very solid shell highly variable in colour which prefers coarse sand or gravel. On a few suitable beaches it is abundant but most colonies are further offshore.

114 *Mercenaria mercenaria* to about 80mm
: This is the American Clam, originally commercially introduced to several sites such as Southampton Water. There are now several permanent populations.

115 *Timoclea ovata* to 17mm
: And one of the smaller species to be found in the drift line. Most are brown but some fringe populations have patterns or other colours. While it is said to be an offshore species, I know some intertidal colonies.

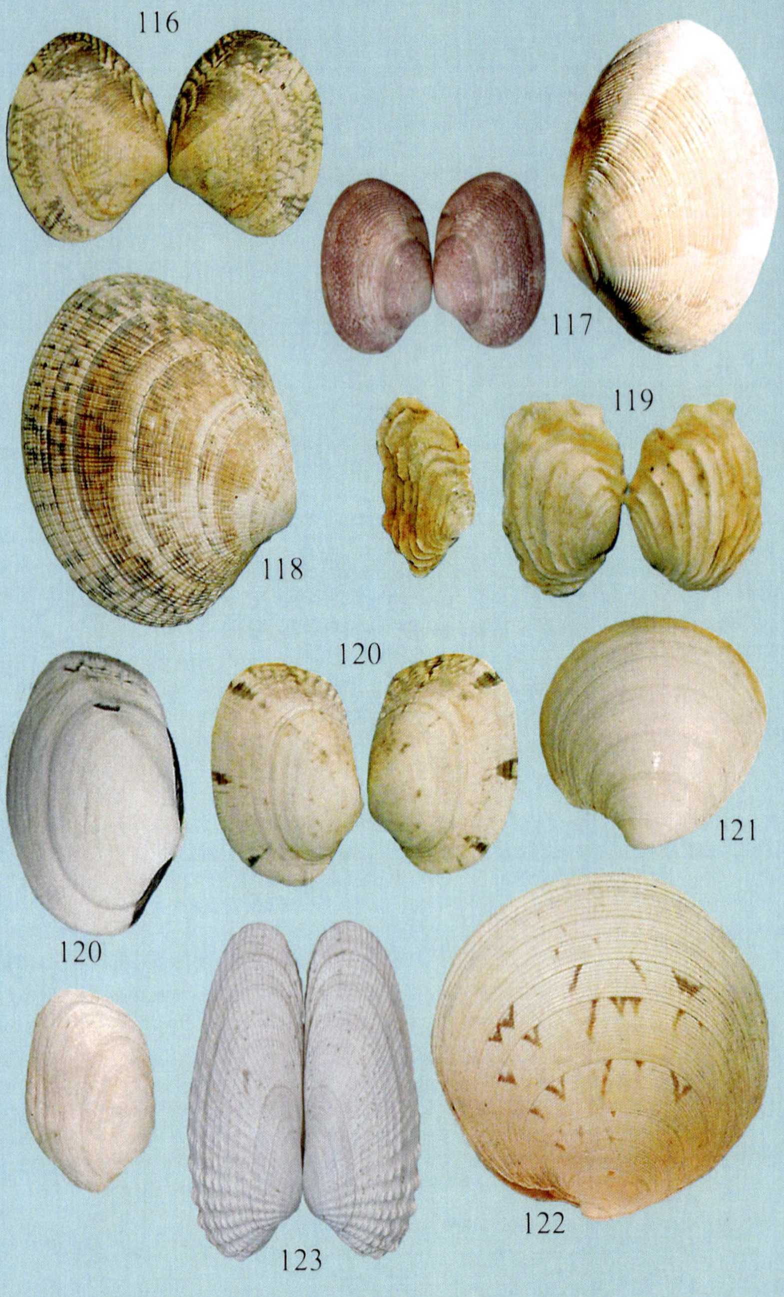
116
117
118
119
120
120
121
122
123

116 *Tapes aureus* (Gmelin, 1791) Carpet Shells
117 *Tapes rhomboides* (Pennant, 1777)
118 *Tapes decussatus* (Linne, 1758)
119 *Irus irus* (Linne, 1758) Irus Venus
120 *Venerupis senegalensis* (Gmelin, 1791) Carpet Shells
121 *Dosinia lupinus* (Linne, 1758)
122 *Dosinia exoleta* (Linne, 1758)
123 *Petricola pholadiformis* Lamarck, 1818 American Piddock

In some, but not all areas, Carpet Shells are attractively coloured. Some years ago, they were collected in Dorset in huge quantities for sale in Spain but, while by no means rare, populations have dropped below the level of commercial viability. Asiatic species are being introduced in the hope that they will breed faster to meet the demand.

116 *Tapes aureus* to 40mm	One of the smaller species, preferring quiet shallow water. The interior can be golden or violet.
117 *Tapes rhomboides* to 66mm	Mainly an offshore species on the mainland but it does live intertidally in the Channel Islands where purple shades are frequent.
118 *Tapes decussatus* to 74mm	This is the largest and most solid of the carpet shells in British waters but foreign examples tend to be smaller. Most are grey but Portland Harbour specimens are more colourful.
119 *Irus irus* to 24mm	Small white shells with pronounced thin ribs, these live in cavities or between stones and develop into distorted shapes. According to some authors the genus is *Notirus*!
120 *Venerupis senegalensis* to 24mm	Formerly known as *Venerupis pullastra*, this attractively patterned shell is common over a wide distribution. Shells that have grown in constricted spaces used to be called *V. saxatilis* but the differences are now discounted.
121 *Dosinia lupinus* to 32mm	Shiny surfaced disc shaped shells smaller than its commoner relation. Invariably white. A deep burrower in fine sand.
122 *Dosinia exoleta* to 56mm	A large burrower in gravel from low intertidal zone down. Some populations have pink tones or chevrons.

Petricola are immigrants from North America but there is a related Mediterranean species.

123 *Petricola pholadiformis* to 56mm	Usually a brilliant white burrower in intertidal soft clay, sometimes with a yellowish periostracum. Some authors say the shell is off white to faun and the periostracum dark brown but I have never seen any like that. Mauve staining can occur in polluted areas.

124

126

125

127

Shell Collecting Made Simple

124 *Mya truncata*	Linne, 1758	Blunt Gaper
125 *Mya arenaria*	Linne, 1758	Soft Shell Clam
126 *Corbula gibba*	(Olivi, 1792)	Basket Shell
127 *Hiatella arctica*	(Linne, 1767)	Saxicave

Mya are normally burrowers but can develop in rock crevices, taking the form of the Cavity. They have leathery tubes to protect the siphons and these often remain attached to dead shells.

124 *Mya truncata*
to 70mm
It normally lives from the lower shore to considerable depths and is common in some areas. Of those I have seen locally, inshore specimens tend to be small.

125 *Mya arenaria*
to 110mm
Another circum-polar species, this tolerates a wide salinity range. Northern specimens are usually more vigorous than those at the Southern end of their range.

Corbula are small shells with unequal valves, one fits inside the other like a lid.

126 *Corbula gibba*
to 14mm
Although this is reported as being one of the commonest bivalves, I have never found many in one place except in the Northern Adriatic. It is said to live on bottoms of silty sand or gravel but my observations do not confirm a consistent pattern.

Hiatella are white bivalves with a brown periostracum. We may have more than one species but this has still to be resolved.

127 *Hiatella arctica*
to 30mm
These filter feeders either occupy cavities in stone or may hang like bunches of grapes, attached by byssus threads below floating docks or other structures. If there does prove to be more than one species involved, I expect the hanging form to be the true *Hiatella arctica*.

128

129

130

131

132

Shell Collecting Made Simple

128 *Pholas dactylus*	Linne, 1758	Piddock or Angels Wings
129 *Barnea candida*	(Linne, 1758)	White Piddock
130 *Barnea parva*	(Pennant, 1777)	Little Piddock
131 *Thracia phaseolina*	(Lamarck, 1818)	Kidneybean Thracia
132 *Pandora inaequivalvis*	(Linne, 1758)	Pandora's Box Shell

Piddocks are borers living in burrows in hard blue clay, soft rocks or peat. They do this by a combination of chemical and abrasive action. In addition to the usual bivalve structure, they have extra plates called protoplaxes to protect the lower gape of the shells.

128 *Pholas dactylus*
to about 150mm

While this is called the Common Piddock and has a wide distribution, I am unconvinced that it is actually as common as literature suggests. Some published data is certainly erroneous. I have found it in hard clay at very low tide on very rare occasions. Dead shells are sometimes lifted as a pair by weed holdfasts and wash ashore.

129 *Barnea candida*
to about 60mm

I have found this to be the commonest of the family, living in hard clay in the lower intertidal zone in the company of *Petricola pholadiformis*. They live vertically. The shape of the shells was consistent. The vent hole is smaller than the waist of the shell. You must break the clay.

130 *Barnea parva*
to about 48mm

This I have only once found alive. Though intertidal they were in a pool and were all tunnelling at 45 degrees from the vertical. They are shorter and broader than *B. candida*. Specimens from dredged blocks of chalk were all short but not consistently shaped.

Thracia are white shells, blunt at the siphonal end, differentiated by size and microsculpture of the outer shell surface. They are said to live in the lower intertidal zone down. I have only ever seen live specimens when offshore dredging.

131 *Thracia phaseolina*
to about 30mm

This is the largest and most frequently found member of the family in British waters. It appears regularly in beach drift in the Channel Islands.

Pandora shells lie on the surface of the sand with the curved side down. Living specimens lie a little offshore where I have found them while wading or snorkelling.

132 *Pandora inaequivalvis*
to about 40mm

The British distribution may be confined to the South and South West of England. It is said to be abundant in a few places but I have not seen more than four on any one day. Dead shells are reflective and easy to spot.

Potential in the UK

The Marine Census addressed 42 sea areas of which five are effectively offshore and five centre on islands or groups of islands. Many islands have potential but not all of them are easy options for us. For instance, 17, "Channel Islands", includes several islands and a huge number of islets and reefs. Herm is exceptional with an impressive range of species and is regularly visited by collectors but some beaches are so good that others escape notice in the general excitement. Sark is much harder collecting with fewer species although individual specimens are often bigger than normal. Guernsey and Jersey have a series of contrasting habitats and a lot of species but they may prove less productive for the inexperienced. The Eastern bays are less attractive than the Western side which is more exposed, but have a better past record. Alderney should be a useful collecting area but it is less visited and I have no direct experience. 19, "Scilly", is particularly useful for bivalves from the shallows between the many islands.

In general the Irish Sea waters, the South and West of Ireland (the edge of several areas follows the 100 fathom line), are fairly well studied and have large numbers of recorded species. While 21, "Bristol Channel" has some quite poor collecting areas; it includes Tenby, Pendine Sands and the Gower, which do yield some brilliant material from time to time. 22, "Cardigan Bay", has some very interesting beaches and species normally further off shore, are deposited. 20, "North Cornwall", is not an easy area but fishermen may have unusual material from deeper water. 18, "Plymouth", is a productive area extending to Penzance, but you will usually be looking for material at extreme low tide. Exciting material falls from crab traps and boats in the small coves along the South Cornwall coast are well worth checking. Once every few years, a fisherman nets a *Charonia*.

16, "Portland", includes South Devon (try Dawlish Warren), West Bay, Portland, Weymouth and most of Dorset. There will always be some material here but luck needs to be on your side as well, if you are to get real rarities without dredging. The effects of the weather are inconsistent. 15, "Wight", includes Poole Harbour and the Solent as well as the I. of W. itself. I have found these areas a little disappointing though in the right conditions, interesting things will turn up. The best is sublittoral. Try dredge sampling using really robust gear.

14, "East Channel", has few really attractive collecting beaches though the material is there offshore waiting for the right storm to move it. Area 13, "Thames", has areas with huge populations but some of these have limited diversity. Sandwich Flats in Kent are usually very productive and rarities are beached from time to time. This is one of the few areas where you have the chance of live *Neptunea* and *Cultellus* on the shore. The cleaner parts of the South bank of the Thames have always been famous for native oysters and other interesting material can be found though the potential for rarities is limited. The North Essex shoreline is more interesting as there are extensive hard clay beds at spring low tide. These have borers and small Turrids at the edges. Small *Epitonium* arrive in the drift line at Frinton-on-Sea.

Worn *Buccinum* make up the bulk of deposited dead shells but one also finds a range of bivalves and other gastropods. Walton and the "Naze" are areas where coastal erosion is being resisted. There are sand beaches and washed out fossils reach the drift line. Broken sea defences provide hard rock habitats where these would not otherwise exist. Sea Areas 12, "Wash", and 13, "Yorkshire", have lower recorded species diversity than the South and West but there can be vast numbers of bivalves. These areas probably need better investigation. As you move further North through 9, "Northumberland", and 7 "Firth of Forth" you find more cold water species. I feel these areas have not yet been comprehensively worked and there must be many as yet unreported species. 6 "Aberdeen", and 5 "Moray Firth", have been less studied and there are some apparent gaps in the distribution records, which will surely be filled in time. These are areas where incoming fishing boats have dumped net cleanings into the sea and have probably accidentally transplanted new colonies. Some of the more interesting Trophons can be found in these waters.

3, "Orkney", 2, "Sutherland", and 1, "Shetland", have traditionally produced some fantastic material but need a major investment in time to update local knowledge. A few collectors have managed to get there for short holidays in recent years but, again, there is still plenty of work to do! 30, "Minch", is a huge area. I have only visited a few parts of it but even the shell sand is exciting and some common species have distinct regional forms. There are stepped seamounts with brilliant material to be had if you dive. You do need a wet suit, even in summer. Wet suits reduce the area that mosquitos and horse flies can get at too!

29, "Clyde and Argyle", The East Coast of Skye is certainly a place where a wet suit is virtually essential as the water can be bitterly cold even in August. This is one of the few areas where you can hope to get *Chlamys nivea* and the best will be in a few feet of water. Calgary Bay on Mull is worth a visit just for the shell sand. I am unaware of any recent serious dredging in the various sea lochs but 19th Century samples yielded a wonderful range of material. Moving South through Seas Area 28, "Belfast", 26, "Isle of Man", and 25, "Solway", high numbers of species have been recorded. Individual specimens are larger than further South. The area deserves a separate book. 24, "Liverpool Bay", is an interesting area where the distribution records are distorted by trawler waste being dumped.

About the Author

Born in Essex in 1944, I learned to walk, on beaches still littered with the debris of war, at Walton-on the-Naze. We collected and ate just about any Gastropod except limpets but I did not take shells seriously at the time. My real interest was sparked by the gift of a batch of beached shells from Sharjah. Key events were the finding of an *Epitonium*, a visit to Herm Island and a close look at a rock at Lloret del Mar.

I discovered the Conchological Society and the British Shell Collectors Club in the mid 1970s. I am a past Secretary and President of the BSCC, a past President of the National Capital Shell Club, Washington DC and had a close association with the Smithsonian Institute, where I assessed projects for grant funding. I am the author of a number of articles, papers and a couple of books, translated into five languages. I have extensive field experience in the UK and from Norway to Aqaba. In the Atlantic I have collected from the Canaries, Portuguese West Africa, the Gambia and from Maine to Belize on the other side of the water. I was privileged to liaise with many of the authorities of the day such as Harold Rehder, Joe Rosewater, Jurgen Knudsen, Fritz Nordsieck, Tom Pain, all now sadly deceased, and with many others still living. I was also granted access to the specialist non-public libraries and collections at the Smithsonian Institute, the National Museum of Wales and the BMNH with their type material. Kathy Way deserves a special mention. I have a reference collection of Atlantic and Mediterranean material plus a lot of other items I cannot bring myself to part with!

Glossary

Anal Canal: A groove or extension of the shell at the rear of the aperture.

Aperture: The mouth of the shell, sometimes sealed with an operculum.

Apex: The pointed end of a Gastropod, often topped by a proto-conch.

Bivalves: Sometimes called Pelecepods. Shells of two plates, usually joined by ligament and/or hinges. A few have additional plates to protect a gaping end.

Byssus: An anchor thread produced by mussels, Pinna and some others. In the ancient Mediterranean, this was woven for expensive fabric.

Cillae. Filaments used to wave or direct potential food particles to the mouth.

Complex: A word used by some experts to cover closely related groups that they cannot confidently divide into species.

Dorsal/ventral: In life, the upper and lower edges of a bivalve.

Foot: The part of a Gastropod with which it crawls, climbs or burrows.

Gastropod: A snail or slug, a creature which crawls on its stomach.

Genus: A closely related family grouping of species, often split into Sub-Genera.

Hinge: Point of connection for bivalves, usually with interlocking teeth and ligament.

Mantle: Extensions of the body which can surround and camouflage the actual shell. This ensures that some species remain smooth and shiny.

Muscle scars: The attachment points for the muscles which open or close bivalves.

Operculum: A horny or "ceramic" plate used by a Gastropod to seal the aperture.

Pelagic: Living in mid ocean driving with the plankton.

Protoconch: The first part of a gastropod to be formed, usually inside the egg, these often fall off adults.

Pteropods: Pelagic "sea butterflies" with white or translucent shells sometimes found in drift lines.

Radula: A series of abrasive plates used to rasp vegetation from rock or drill holes in other shells.

Radula Dart: An adaptation of the radula to inject poison to subdue prey.

Scapholopod: Often called "tusk shells", these have curved, tubular shells.

Siphonal Canal: The extension of shell shielding the siphons of Gastropods.

Siphons: Extendable tubes; bivalves for filter feeding or Gastropod sensory organs.

Species: An artificial concept to link members of the same gene pool which interbreed. Biology is probably the only branch of science where the basic unit of definition is not universally agreed or understood!

Taxa, Taxon: Nomenclature and components of the Latin names of species.

Umbilicus: The hole or depression at the centre of the spiral of growth.

Varix: A thickened axial lip or ridge marking a growth stage.

Index

Abra **84, 85**
Acanthocardia **74, 75, 76, 77**
Acid 21, 22, 28
Acteon **66, 67**
Aequipecten **72, 73**
Animal Diagrams **41, 42**
Angulus **82, 83**
Anomia **74, 75**
Antalis **66, 67**
Aporrhais **58, 59**
Aquaria 16
Arca **68, 69**
Arctica **84, 85**
Ark Shells **68, 69**

Barnea **42**, 92, **93**
Beach "Nourishment" 15
Bittersweets **68, 69**
BMNH 38
Boats 15
Boulders 10
Bubble Shells **66, 67**
Buccinum **62, 63**

Calyptrea **58, 59**
Capulus **58, 59**
Carpet Shells **88, 89**
Chamalea **86, 87**
Chemo-signalling 36
Chitons 5, 10, **50, 51**
Chlamys **72, 73**
Clausinella **86, 87**
Cleaning 21, 24
Clubs 48
Coat of Mail Shells **50, 51**
Cockles 8, **74, 75, 76, 77**
Collecting Methods 17
Colours 22
Colus 42, **64, 65**
Comarmondia 41, **66, 67**,
Conservation 26
Coralline Algae 11
Corbula **90, 91**
Crab Boats 15
Crasostrea **70, 71**
Crepidula **58, 59**

Data 25, 20
Detergent Kills 14
Dog Whelks **62, 63**
Donax **82, 83**
Dosinia **88, 89**
Dredges 28, **44, 45**
Drift line 3
Driftwood 13

Emarginula **50, 51**
Ensis 3, **80, 81**
Epitonium 8, **60, 61**
Equipment 27
Erosion/ Run off Channels 4
Estuaries 6
Exchanging 32
Exotics 29
Experts 18
Ex-astropecten 13
Ex-pisces 13, **73**

Fabulina **82, 83**
File Shells **70, 71**
Fishermen's Waste 14
Fishmongers 14

Gari **42, 85, 86**
Gastronomy 34
Gastropods **41**, 101
Gibbula **54, 55**
Glossary 101
Glycymeris **68, 69**
Gouldia **86, 87**
Gravel 5, 10
Haliotis **50, 51**
Haminoea **66, 67**
Harbour Repairs 15
Hard Clay 6
Hard Coral 12

Hazards ... 19, 45
Helcion ... 11, **52, 53**
Hermit Crabs ... 15, 26
Heteranomia ... **74, 75**
Hiatella ... **90, 91**
Hinia ... **41, 64, 65**

ICZNS ... 37
Irus ... **88, 89**

Kelp ... 11
Keyhole Limpets ... **50, 51**

Labelling ... 25, 20
Lagoons ... 4, 5
Landfill ... 15
Learned Societies ... 32, 48, 49
Light ... 24
Limaria ... **70, 71**
Limpets ... 4, **50, 51, 52, 53**
Literature ... 33, 34
Littorina ... **56, 57**
Loripes ... **74, 75**
Lucines ... **74, 75**
Lucinoma ... **74, 75**
Lutraria ... **78, 79**

Macoma ... **82, 83**
Mactra ... **78, 79**
Maerl ... 11
Marine Census ... 25, 95

Marine Charts   28, **39**
Markets   14
Mercenaria   **86, 87**
Micro Shells   5, 23, **43**
Microwave   23, 29
Modiolus   11, **68, 69**
Moerella   **82, 83**
Moonfleet   5
Moon Snails   **60, 61**
Mud   3, 7
Museums   31, 33
Mussels   6, **68, 69**
Mya   **90, 91**

Nassarius   17
Natica   **60, 61**
National Museums   2, 38, 48
Neptunea   7, **64, 65**
Night   16
Nucula   **68, 69**

Observation   18
Ocenebra   **62, 63**
Opercula or Operculum 22, 23, **41**
Ormers   **50. 51**
Ostrea   **70, 71**
Otter Shells   **78, 79**
Oysters   **70, 71**

Paliolum ... 72, 73
Pandora ... **92, 93**
Peat ... 7
Pecten ... 72, 73
Periostracum ... 22, **41, 42**
Petricola ... **88, 89**
Pharus ... **84, 85**
Pholads ... **92, 93**
Piddocks ... **92, 93**
Polinices ... **60, 61**
Pollution ... 14
Posidonia ... 11
Preserving ... 23
Provinces ... 29
Pseudamussium ... 72, 73

Quick Sand ... 4

Razor Shells ... **80, 81**
Restaurants ... 16
Rock Reefs ... 6, **40**
Run-off Channels ... 4

Saddle Oysters ... **74, 75**
Saline Lagoons ... 4, 5
Sand ... 3, 7, **40**
Scallop Factories ... 14
Scallops ... 72, 73
Scaphander ... **66, 67**
Scrobicularia ... **84, 85**
Sea Areas (Marine Census) ... 46, **47**, 95, 96, 97, 98

Shallows … 16, 17
Shell Clubs … 31
Shell Sand/ Grit … 8
Shell Shows … 29, 31
Shingle … 10, 11
Shore Profiles … 40
Siphons … 18, 41
Slit Limpet … **50, 51**
Soft Corals … 12
Solen … **80, 81**
Sorting … 8
Splash Zone … 17
Spisula … **78, 79**
Sponges … 12
Strandline … 17, 3
Sublittoral … 40
Sunset Shells … **84, 85**
Surf Clams … **78, 79**

Tapes … **88, 89**
Taxon … 35
Taxonomy … 2, 35
Tectura … **50, 51**
Tellins … **82, 83**
Tentacles … 18
Thracia … **92, 93**
Tides … 3, 18, **40**
Timoclea … **86, 87**
Top Shells … **54, 55**
Transporting … 24
Traps … 16

Tricolia	**54, 55**
Trivia	**58, 59**
Turrids	**66, 67**
Turritella	**56, 57**
Tusk Shells	**66, 67**
Types	35
Vacuum Jar	28
Values	30
Velutina	**60, 61**
Venerupis	**88, 89**
Venus Shells	8, **86, 87, 88, 89**
Weed	9
Weed Washings	9
Wentletraps	**60, 61**
Winkles	**56, 57**
Zostera	5, 9, 26

Logic behind this index: Latin names and components thereof are in italics unless the word has been anglicised by addition of extra letters or incorporation within a compound word. Bold type indicates a page where a relevant illustration is found plus the text directly linked with the illustration. Normal type numerals are significant pages of reference only, as many names will exist in secondary roles over a very large number of pages